MATTHEW
for
EVERYONE

PART 1
CHAPTERS 1—15

N. T. (Tom) Wright is Canon Theologian of Westminster Abbey, and holds the degree of Doctor of Divinity from Oxford University and an honorary DD from Aberdeen University. He taught New Testament Studies in Cambridge, Montreal and Oxford, and worked as a college chaplain, before becoming Dean of Lichfield in 1994 and moving to Westminster in 2000. He has written over thirty books about the origins of Christianity and its contemporary relevance. Dr Wright broadcasts regularly on radio and television. He is married with four young adult children.

MATTHEW
for
EVERYONE

PART 1
CHAPTERS 1—15

TOM
WRIGHT

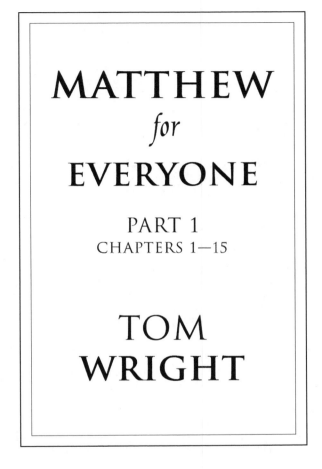

SPCK

Westminster John Knox Press

First published in Great Britain by
Society for Promoting Christian Knowledge
36 Causton Street
London SW1P 4ST

Second edition copublished in 2004 by the Society for Promoting
Christian Knowledge, London, and Westminster John Knox Press,
Louisville, KY 40202.

06 07 08 09 10 11 12 13 — 10 9 8 7 6 5 4

British Library Cataloguing-in-Publication Data
A catalogue record for this book is available from the British Library.

ISBN-13: 978-0-281-05301-8; ISBN-10: 0-281-05301-4 (U.K. edition)

United States Library of Congress Cataloging-in-Publication Data
is on file at the Library of Congress, Washington, D.C.

ISBN-13: 978-0-664-22786-9; ISBN-10: 0-664-22786-4 (U.S. edition)

Typeset by Pioneer Associates, Perthshire
Printed in Great Britain at
Ashford Colour Press
Reprinted in the United States
of America by Versa

CONTENTS

CONTENTS

CONTENTS

For

Christopher Philip Unwin,

priest and teacher of the faith,
with gratitude for the love, support and prayers
of over fifty years

INTRODUCTION

On the very first occasion when someone stood up in public to tell people about Jesus, he made it very clear: this message is for *everyone*.

It was a great day – sometimes called the birthday of the church. The great wind of God's spirit had swept through Jesus' followers and filled them with a new joy and a sense of God's presence and power. Their leader, Peter, who only a few weeks before had been crying like a baby because he'd lied and cursed and denied even knowing Jesus, found himself on his feet explaining to a huge crowd that something had happened which had changed the world for ever. What God had done for him, Peter, he was beginning to do for the whole world: new life, forgiveness, new hope and power were opening up like spring flowers after a long winter. A new age had begun in which the living God was going to do new things in the world – beginning then and there with the individuals who were listening to him. 'This promise is for *you*,' he said, 'and for your children, and for everyone who is far away' (Acts 2.39). It wasn't just for the person standing next to you. It was for everyone.

Within a remarkably short time this came true to such an extent that the young movement spread throughout much of the known world. And one way in which the *everyone* promise worked out was through the writings of the early Christian leaders. These short works – mostly letters and stories about Jesus – were widely circulated and eagerly read. They were never intended for either a religious or intellectual elite. From the very beginning they were meant for everyone.

That is as true today as it was then. Of course, it matters that some people give time and care to the historical evidence, the meaning of the original words (the early Christians wrote in Greek), and the exact and particular force of what different writers were saying about God, Jesus, the world and themselves. This series is based quite closely on that sort of work. But the point of it all is that the message can get out to everyone, especially to people who wouldn't normally read a book with footnotes and Greek words in it. That's the sort of person for whom these books are written. And that's why there's a glossary, in the back, of the key words that you can't really get along without, with a simple description of what they mean. Whenever you see a word in **bold type** in the text, you can go to the back and remind yourself what's going on.

There are of course many translations of the New Testament available today. The one I offer here is designed for the same kind of reader: one who mightn't necessarily understand the more formal, sometimes even ponderous, tones of some of the standard ones. I have of course tried to keep as close to the original as I can. But my main aim has been to be sure that the words can speak not just to some people, but to everyone.

Matthew's gospel presents Jesus in a rich, many-sided way. He appears as the Messiah of Israel, the king who will rule and save the world. He comes before us as the Teacher greater even than Moses. And, of course, he is presented as the son of man giving his life for us all. Matthew lays it all out step by step and invites us to learn the wisdom of the gospel message and the new way of life that results from it. So here it is: Matthew for everyone!

Tom Wright

PALESTINE
In New Testament
times

Tyre

Caesarea
Philippi

SYRO-
PHOENICIA

SYRIA

Ptolemais

Chorazin
Capernaum
Gennesaret

Bethsaida

Sea of Galilee

Gergesa?

MT CARMEL

Tiberias

Cana

Nazareth

Nain

Gadara

DECAPOLIS

Plain
of Esdraelon

Mediterranean Sea

Caesarea

Salim
Aenon

Plain of Sharon

Samaria

SAMARIA

Sychar

Gerasa

River Jordan

MT GERIZIM

Antipatris

Arimathea

Ephraim

Joppa

Lydda

Jericho

Bethany-
beyond-Jordan

Emmaus

Jerusalem

Bethphage

Azotus

Bethany

JUDAEA

Qumran

Askelon

Bethlehem

Wilderness of Judaea

Dead Sea

Hebron

Gaza

IDUMEA

NABATAEA

Beersheba

Jesus' Genealogy

¹This book contains the family tree of Jesus the Messiah, the son of David, the son of Abraham.

²Abraham was the father of Isaac, Isaac of Jacob, Jacob of Judah and his brothers, ³Judah of Peres and Zara by Tamar, Peres of Esrom, Esrom of Aram, ⁴Aram of Aminadab, Aminadab of Naason, Naason of Salmon, ⁵Salmon of Boaz by Rahab, Boaz of Obed by Ruth, Obed of Jesse, ⁶and Jesse of David the king.

David was the father of Solomon (by the wife of Uriah), ⁷Solomon of Rehoboam, Rehoboam of Abijah, Abijah of Asaph, ⁸Asaph of Jehosaphat, Jehosaphat of Joram, Joram of Uzziah, ⁹Uzziah of Joatham, Joatham of Ahaz, Ahaz of Hezekiah, ¹⁰Hezekiah of Manasseh, Manasseh of Amoz, Amoz of Josiah, ¹¹Josiah of Jeconiah and his brothers, at the time of the exile in Babylon.

¹²After the Babylonian exile, Jeconiah became the father of Salathiel, Salathiel of Zerubbabel, ¹³Zerubbabel of Abioud, Abioud of Eliakim, Eliakim of Azor, ¹⁴Azor of Sadok, Sadok of Achim, Achim of Elioud, ¹⁵Elioud of Eleazar, Eleazar of Matthan, Matthan of Jacob, ¹⁶and Jacob of Joseph the husband of Mary, from whom was born Jesus, who is called 'Messiah'.

¹⁷So all the generations from Abraham to David add up to fourteen; from David to the Babylonian exile, fourteen generations; and from the Babylonian exile to the Messiah, fourteen generations.

In Oscar Wilde's play *The Importance of Being Earnest*, the hero is asked about his family background, and is forced to confess that he had lost both his parents. He had been found, as a tiny baby, in a handbag. The indignation that greets these revelations is one of the most famous (and funny) moments in all Wilde's work. As one of them comments, 'To lose one parent . . . may be regarded as a misfortune; to lose both looks like carelessness.'

The point is, of course, that tracing one's family pedigree is regarded by many societies as enormously important. Even in the liberal, democratic, Western world, where ideas of equality have long been cherished, tracing one's family roots provides a sense of identity which many find exciting and encouraging. In many more traditional societies, such as parts of Africa, or the Maori culture in New Zealand, family histories and family trees are a vital part of who you are. And of course, in tight-knit families and tribes that have lasted for centuries, there will be a good deal of intermarrying, so that the same person can often trace their descent several different ways. In such a world, telling the story of one's ancestry is as important a way of disclosing one's identity as producing a good curriculum vitae is when job-hunting in the modern world.

This should remind us what is going on at the beginning of Matthew's **gospel**. The average modern person who thinks 'maybe I'll read the New Testament' is puzzled to find, on the very first page, a long list of names he or she has never heard of. But it is important not to think that this is a waste of time. For many cultures ancient and modern, and certainly in the Jewish world of Matthew's day, this genealogy was the equivalent of a roll of drums, a fanfare of trumpets, and a town crier calling for attention. Any first-century Jew would find this family tree both impressive and compelling. Like a great procession coming down a city street, we watch the figures at the front, and the ones in the middle, but all eyes are waiting for the one who comes in the position of greatest honour, right at the end.

Matthew has arranged the names so as to make this point even clearer. Most Jews, telling the story of Israel's ancestry, would begin with Abraham; but only a select few, by the first century AD, would trace their own line through King David. Even fewer would be able to continue by going on through Solomon and the other kings of Judah all the way to the **exile**.

For most of the time after the Babylonian exile, Israel had not had a functioning monarchy. The kings and queens they had had in the last 200 years before the birth of Jesus were not from David's family. Herod the Great, the old king we shall presently meet, had no royal blood, and was not even fully Jewish, but was simply an opportunist military commander whom the Romans made into a king to further their own Middle Eastern agendas. But there were some who knew that they were descended from the line of true and ancient kings. Even to tell that story, to list those names, was therefore making a political statement. You wouldn't want Herod's spies to over-hear you boasting that you were part of the true royal family.

But that's what Matthew does, on Jesus' behalf. And, as though to emphasize that Jesus isn't just one member in an ongoing family, but actually the goal of the whole list, he arranges the genealogy into three groups of 14 names – or, perhaps we should say, into six groups of seven names. The number seven was and is one of the most powerful symbolic numbers, and to be born at the beginning of the seventh seven in the sequence is clearly to be the climax of the whole list. This birth, Matthew is saying, is what Israel has been waiting for for two thousand years.

The particular markers along the way also tell their story. Abraham is the founding father, to whom God made great promises. He would be given the land of Canaan, and the nations would be blessed through his family. David was the great king, to whom, again, God made promises of future lordship over the whole world. The Babylonian exile was the time when it seemed that all these promises were lost for ever, drowned in the sea of Israel's sins and God's judgment. But the prophets of the exile promised that God would again restore Abraham's people and David's royal line. The long years that followed, during which some of the Jews had come back from Babylon but were still living under foreign, pagan

3

oppression, were seen by many as a continuing 'exile', still waiting for God to deliver Israel from sin and the judgment it brought. Now is the moment, Matthew is saying, for all this to happen. The child who comes at the end of this line is God's anointed, the long-awaited **Messiah**, to fulfil all the layers and levels of the prophecies of old.

But Matthew also knows that the way it has happened is very strange. He is about to tell how Mary, Jesus' mother, had become pregnant not through her fiancé, Joseph, but through the **holy spirit**. So Matthew adds to his list reminders of the strange ways God worked in the royal family itself: Judah treating his daughter-in-law Tamar as a prostitute, Boaz being the son of the Jericho prostitute Rahab, and David committing adultery with the wife of Uriah the Hittite. If God can work through these bizarre ways, he seems to be saying, watch what he's going to do now.

Matthew's gospel has stood at the front of the New Testament since very early times. Millions of Christians have read this genealogy as the beginning of their own exploration of who Jesus was and is. Once we understand what it all means, we are ready to proceed with the story. This, Matthew is saying, is *both* the fulfilment of two millennia of God's promises and purposes *and* something quite new and different. God still works like that today: keeping his promises, acting in character, and yet always ready with surprises for those who learn to trust him.

MATTHEW 1.18–25

The Birth of Jesus

[18]This was how the birth of Jesus the Messiah took place. His mother, Mary, was engaged to Joseph; but before they came together she turned out to be pregnant – by the holy spirit. [19]Joseph, her husband-to-be, was an upright man. He didn't

want to make a public example of her. So he decided to set the marriage aside privately. ²⁰But, while he was considering this, an angel of the Lord suddenly appeared to him in a dream.

'Joseph, son of David,' the angel said, 'Don't be afraid to get married to Mary. The child she is carrying is from the holy spirit. ²¹She is going to have a son. You must give him the name Jesus; he is the one who will save his people from their sins.'

²²All this happened so that what the Lord said through the prophet might be fulfilled: ²³'Look: the virgin is pregnant, and will have a son, and they shall give him the name Emmanuel,' – which means, in translation, 'God with us.'

²⁴When Joseph woke up from his sleep he did what the Lord's angel had told him to. He married his wife, ²⁵but he didn't have sexual relations with her until after the birth of her son. And he gave him the name Jesus.

One of the most memorable movies I have seen is the film of Charles Dickens's novel *Little Dorrit*. It is actually two films, both very long. The two films don't follow in sequence, telling the first and second halves of the story; instead, each film shows the whole drama, but from a different point of view. First we see the action through the eyes of the hero; then, in the second film, the same story through the eyes of the heroine. A few scenes are identical, but in the second film we understand many things that hadn't been clear first time around. Like seeing with two eyes instead of one, the double movie enables the viewer to get a sense of depth and perspective on the whole dramatic story.

The story of Jesus' birth in Matthew's **gospel** is seen through the eyes of Joseph; in Luke's gospel, we see it through Mary's. No attempt is made to bring them into line. The central fact is the same; but instead of Luke's picture of an excited Galilean girl, learning that she is to give birth to God's **Messiah**, Matthew shows us the more sober Joseph, discovering that his fiancée is pregnant. The only point where the two stories come close is when the angel says to Joseph, as Gabriel said to Mary, 'Don't be afraid.' That is an important word for us, too, as we read the accounts of Jesus' birth.

Fear at this point is normal. For centuries now many opponents of Christianity, and many devout Christians themselves, have felt that these stories are embarrassing and unnecessary – and untrue. We know (many will say) that **miracles** don't happen. Remarkable healings, perhaps; there are ways of explaining them. But not babies born without human fathers. This is straining things too far.

Some go further. These stories, they say, have had an unfortunate effect. They have given the impression that sex is dirty and that God doesn't want anything to do with it. They have given rise to the legend that Mary stayed a virgin for ever (something the Bible never says; indeed, here and elsewhere it implies that she and Joseph lived a normal married life after Jesus' birth). This has promoted the belief that virginity is better than marriage. And so on.

It is of course true that strange ideas have grown up around the story of Jesus' conception and birth, but Matthew (and Luke) can hardly be blamed for that. They were telling the story they believed was both true and the ultimate explanation of why Jesus was the person he was.

They must have known that they were taking a risk. In the ancient pagan world there were plenty of stories of heroes conceived by the intervention of a god, without a human father. Surely Matthew, with his very Jewish perspective on everything, would hardly invent such a thing, or copy it from someone else unless he really believed it? Wouldn't it be opening Christianity to the sneers of its opponents, who would quickly suggest the obvious alternative, namely that Mary had become pregnant through some more obvious but less reputable means?

Well, yes, it would; but that would only be relevant if nobody already knew that there had been something strange about Jesus' conception. In John's gospel we hear the echo of a taunt made during Jesus' lifetime: maybe, the crowds suggest, Jesus' mother had been misbehaving before her marriage (8.41). It looks as though Matthew and Luke are telling this story because they know rumours have circulated and they want to set the record straight.

Alternatively, people have suggested that Matthew made his story up so that it would present a 'fulfilment' of the passage he quotes in verse 23, from Isaiah 7.14. But, interestingly, there is no evidence that anyone before Matthew saw that verse as something that would have to be fulfilled by the coming Messiah. It looks rather as though he found the verse because he already knew the story, not the other way round.

Everything depends, of course, on whether you believe that the living God could, or would, act like that. Some say he couldn't ('miracles don't happen'); others that he wouldn't ('if he did that, why doesn't he intervene to stop genocide?'). Some say Joseph, and others at the time, didn't know the scientific laws of nature the way we do – though this story gives the lie to that, since if Joseph hadn't known how babies were normally made he wouldn't have had a problem with Mary's unexpected pregnancy.

But Matthew and Luke don't ask us to take the story all by itself. They ask us to see it in the light both of the entire history of Israel – in which God was always present and at work, often in very surprising ways – and, more particularly, of the subsequent story of Jesus himself. Does the rest of the story, and the impact of Jesus on the world and countless individuals within it ever since, make it more or less likely that he was indeed conceived by a special act of the **holy spirit**?

That is a question everyone must answer for themselves. But Matthew wouldn't want us to stop there. He wants to tell us more about who Jesus was and is, in a time-honoured Jewish fashion: by his special names. The name 'Jesus' was a popular boys' name at the time, being in Hebrew the same as 'Joshua', who brought the Israelites into the promised land after the death of Moses. Matthew sees Jesus as the one who will now complete what the **law** of Moses pointed to but could not of itself produce. He will rescue his people, not from slavery in Egypt, but from the slavery of sin, the **'exile'** they have suffered not just in Babylon but in their own hearts and lives.

By contrast, the name 'Emmanuel', mentioned in Isaiah 7.14 and 8.8, was not given to anyone else, perhaps because it would say more about a child than anyone would normally dare. It means 'God with us'. Matthew's whole gospel is framed by this theme: at the very end, Jesus promises that he will be 'with' his people to the close of the age (28.20). The two names together express the meaning of the story. God is present, with his people; he doesn't 'intervene' from a distance, but is always active, sometimes in most unexpected ways. And God's actions are aimed at rescuing people from a helpless plight, demanding that he take the initiative and do things people had regarded as (so to speak) inconceivable.

This is the God, and this is the Jesus, whose story Matthew will now set before us. This is the God, and this is the Jesus, who comes to us still today when human possibilities have run out, offering new and startling ways forward, in fulfilment of his promises, by his powerful love and grace.

MATTHEW 2.1–12

The Magi Visit Jesus

¹When Jesus was born, in Bethlehem of Judaea, at the time when Herod was king, some wise and learned men came to Jerusalem from the East.

²'Where is the one,' they asked, 'who has been born to be

king of the Jews? We have seen his star in the east, and we have come to worship him.'

³When King Herod heard this, he was very disturbed, and the whole of Jerusalem was as well. ⁴He called together all the chief priests and scribes of the people, and enquired from them where the Messiah was to be born.

⁵'In Bethlehem of Judaea,' they replied. 'That's what it says in the prophet:

⁶You, Bethlehem, in Judah's land
are not the least of Judah's princes;
from out of you will come the ruler
who will shepherd Israel my people.'

⁷Then Herod called the wise men to him in secret. He found out from them precisely when the star had appeared. ⁸Then he sent them to Bethlehem.

'Off you go,' he said, 'and make a thorough search for the child. When you find him, report back to me, so that I can come and worship him too.'

⁹When they heard what the king said, they set off. There was the star, the one they had seen in the east, going ahead of them! It went and stood still over the place where the child was. ¹⁰When they saw the star, they were beside themselves with joy and excitement. ¹¹They went into the house and saw the child, with Mary his mother, and they fell down and worshipped him. They opened their treasure-chests, and gave him presents: gold, frankincense and myrrh.

¹²They were warned in a dream not to go back to Herod. So they returned to their own country by a different route.

I was convinced it was a helicopter. It was a dark night, and a bright light was shining just above the nearby town. Surely, I thought, the police must be out looking for a criminal; or perhaps there had been an accident. We had just come from the city, and our eyes weren't yet adjusted for the dark night-time out in the country. But there, plain for all to see, was a light in the sky: a bright, almost dazzling light that could only have come, I was convinced, from a man-made searchlight attached to an aeroplane or helicopter.

But I was wrong, as our taxi-driver took delight in pointing out to me. It was the planet Venus. It was at one of its closest points to our planet, Earth; it was hanging in the evening sky, brighter than I would ever have imagined. My eyes were too used to the city streetlights. I had forgotten just how bright, and how beautiful and evocative, the night sky can be.

The ancient world, innocent of streetlights, never forgot the night sky. Many people, particularly in the countries to the east of Palestine, had developed the study of the stars and the planets to a fine art, giving each one very particular meanings. They believed, after all, that the whole world was of a piece; everything was interconnected, and when something important was happening on earth you could expect to see it reflected in the heavens. Alternatively, a remarkable event among the stars and planets must mean, they thought, a remarkable event on earth.

Scholars have laboured to discover what Matthew's 'star' might have been. Halley's Comet appeared in 12–11 BC, but that would be very early for this story. Or it could have been some kind of supernova. More likely is the fact that the planets Jupiter and Saturn were in conjunction with each other three times in 7 BC. Since Jupiter was the 'royal' or kingly planet, and Saturn was sometimes thought to represent the Jews, the conclusion was obvious: a new king of the Jews was about to be born. We cannot be certain if this was why the 'wise and learned men' came from the East. But, even if it wasn't, nothing is more likely than that thoughtful astronomers or astrologers (the two went together in the ancient world), noticing strange events in the heavens, would search out their earthly counterparts. If, as it appears, they were also wealthy, they would have no major difficulty in making the journey.

Matthew is not telling us all this simply to satisfy astronomical curiosity. Nor is he offering us the kind of cosy, picture-book story we have created for ourselves out of it, with strange but gentle oriental kings bringing gifts to a child in a stable. (Matthew says nothing about a stable; as far as we know from his **gospel**, Mary and Joseph were simply living in Bethlehem at the time, only moving to Nazareth later (2.23). Nor does he say the visitors were themselves royal.) The overtones of his story are quite different.

What he tells us is political dynamite. Jesus, Matthew is saying, is the true king of the Jews, and old Herod is the false one, a usurper, an impostor. As we shall see, this Herod died soon after Jesus' birth; but his sons ruled on, and one of them, Herod Antipas, plays a significant role in the developing story of Jesus himself. The house of Herod did not take kindly to the idea of anyone else claiming to be 'king of the Jews'.

The arrival of the 'Magi' (that's the word Matthew uses for them; it can refer to 'magicians', or 'astrologers', or experts in interpreting dreams, portents and other strange happenings) introduces us to something which Matthew wants us to be clear about from the start. If Jesus is in some sense king of the Jews, that doesn't mean that his rule is limited to the Jewish people. At the heart of many prophecies about the coming king, the **Messiah**, there were predictions that his rule would bring God's justice and peace to the whole world (e.g. Psalm 72; Isaiah 11.1–10). Matthew will end his gospel with Jesus commissioning his followers to go out and make **disciples** from every nation; this, it seems, is the way that the prophecies of the Messiah's worldwide rule are going to come true. There are hints of the same thing at various points in the gospel (e.g. 8.11), though Jesus himself did not deliberately seek out **Gentiles** during his ministry (see 10.5–6). But here, even when Jesus is an apparently unknown baby, there is a sign of what is to come. The gifts that the Magi brought were the sort of

11

things that people in the ancient world would think of as appropriate presents to bring to kings, or even gods.

There is another way as well in which this story points ahead to the climax of the gospel. Jesus will finally come face to face with the representative of the world's greatest king – Pilate, Caesar's subordinate. Pilate will have rather different gifts to give him, though he, too, is warned by a dream not to do anything to him (27.19). His soldiers are the first Gentiles since the Magi to call Jesus 'king of the Jews' (27.29), but the crown they give him is made of thorns, and his throne is a cross. At that moment, instead of a bright star, there will be an unearthly darkness (27.45), out of which we shall hear a single Gentile voice: yes, he really was God's son (27.54).

Listen to the whole story, Matthew is saying. Think about what it meant for Jesus to be the true king of the Jews. And then – come to him, by whatever route you can, and with the best gifts you can find.

MATTHEW 2.13–23

Travels to Egypt

[13]After the Magi had gone, suddenly an angel of the Lord appeared to Joseph in a dream.

'Get up,' he said, 'and take the child, and his mother, and hurry off to Egypt. Stay there until I tell you. Herod is going to hunt for the child, to kill him.'

[14]So he got up and took the child and his mother by night, and went off to Egypt. [15]He stayed there until the death of Herod. This happened to fulfil what the Lord said through the prophet:

Out of Egypt I called my son.

[16]When Herod saw that he had been tricked by the Magi, he flew into a towering rage. He dispatched people to kill all the

boys in Bethlehem, and in all its surrounding districts, from two years old and under, according to the time the Magi had told him. [17]That was when the word that came through Jeremiah the prophet was fulfilled:

[18]There was heard a voice in Rama,
Crying and loud lamentation.
Rachel is weeping for her children,
And will not let anyone comfort her,
Because they are no more.

[19]After the death of Herod, suddenly an angel of the Lord appeared in a dream to Joseph in Egypt.

[20]'Get up,' he said, 'and take the child and his mother and go to the land of Israel. Those who wanted to kill the child are dead.'

[21]So he got up, took the child and his mother, and went to the land of Israel.

[22]But when he heard that Archelaus was ruling Judaea instead of his father Herod, he was afraid to go back there. After being advised in a dream, he went off to the region of Galilee. [23]When he got there, he settled in a town called Nazareth. This was to fulfil what the prophet had spoken:

He shall be called a Nazorean.

I was once preaching at a big Christmas service where a well-known historian, famous for his scepticism towards Christianity, had been persuaded to attend by his family. Afterwards, he approached me, all smiles.

'I've finally worked out', he declared, 'why people like Christmas.'

'Really?' I said. 'Do tell me.'

'A baby threatens no one,' he said, 'so the whole thing is a happy event which means nothing at all!'

I was dumbfounded. At the heart of the Christmas story in

Matthew's **gospel** is a baby who poses such a threat to the most powerful man around that he kills a whole village full of other babies in order to try to get rid of him. At the heart of the Christmas story in Luke, too, is a baby who, if only the Roman emperor knew it, will be Lord of the whole world. Within a generation his followers will be persecuted by the empire as a danger to good order. Whatever else you say about Jesus, from his birth onwards, people certainly found him a threat. He upset their power-games, and suffered the usual fate of people who do that.

In fact, the shadow of the cross falls over the story from this moment on. Jesus is born with a price on his head. Plots are hatched; angels have to warn Joseph; they only just escape from Bethlehem in time. Herod the Great, who thought nothing of killing members of his own family, including his own beloved wife, when he suspected them of scheming against him, and who gave orders when dying that the leading citizens of Jericho should be slaughtered so that people would be weeping at his funeral – this Herod would not bat an eyelid at the thought of killing lots of little babies in case one of them should be regarded as a royal pretender. As his power had increased, so had his paranoia – a not unfamiliar progression, as dictators around the world have shown from that day to this.

The gospel of Jesus the **Messiah** was born, then, in a land and at a time of trouble, tension, violence and fear. Banish all thoughts of peaceful Christmas scenes. Before the Prince of Peace had learned to walk and talk, he was a homeless refugee with a price on his head. At the same time, in this passage and several others Matthew insists that we see in Jesus, even when things are at their darkest, the fulfilment of scripture. This is how Israel's redeemer was to appear; this is how God would set about liberating his people, and bringing justice to the whole world. No point in arriving in comfort, when the world is in misery; no point having an easy life, when the world

14

suffers violence and injustice! If he is to be Emmanuel, God-with-us, he must be with us where the pain is. That's what this chapter is about.

Matthew's quotation of various biblical texts here has puzzled many readers. When he quotes Hosea 11.1 in verse 15 ('Out of Egypt I called my son'), it looks for a moment as though he is ignoring the fact that the prophet was looking back to Israel's **Exodus** from Egypt, not forward to a '**son of God**' yet to come. But this itself ignores the fact that, for Matthew, part of Jesus' role and vocation is precisely to make Israel's story complete: as 'son of God' he is, as it were, Israel-in-person, succeeding at last where Israel had failed (see particularly 4.1–11).

The next quotation, providing a prophetic backdrop to Herod's slaughter of the Bethlehem children (verse 18), is from Jeremiah, and once again there is more to it than meets the eye. The passage in Jeremiah (31.15) is all about God's renewal of the **covenant**, bringing Israel back from **exile** at last. Though Israel must weep and mourn, rescue is on the way. Again, Matthew is hinting that Jesus is bringing deliverance even when everything seems bleak and hopeless.

Finally, Matthew links the settling of the family in Nazareth with the prophecy of Isaiah 11.1. There, the word *nazir* means 'branch'. A branch, says Isaiah, shall grow out of the root of Jesse; in other words, a new beginning will be made for the royal house of David. This is what the whole passage is promising, and Matthew is determined to find hints of it wherever he can. In Jesus, not despite the frantic and tragic events that happened around his birth but because of them, God is providing the salvation and rescue that Israel longed for, and, through that, his justice for the world.

We have not heard the last of the house of Herod. But the young child born to be the true king of the Jews has been introduced as the bearer of God's salvation, and indeed of

God's personal presence. From now on, Matthew invites us to watch as God's new Exodus unfolds before our eyes.

MATTHEW 3.1–10

The Preaching of John the Baptist

¹In those days John the Baptist appeared. He was preaching in the Judaean wilderness.

²'Repent!' he was saying. 'The kingdom of heaven is coming!'

³John, you see, is the person spoken of by Isaiah the prophet, when he said,

> The voice of someone shouting in the desert:
> 'Prepare the route that the Lord will take,
> Straighten out his paths!'

⁴John himself had clothing made from camel's hair, and a leather belt around his waist. His food was locusts and wild honey. ⁵Jerusalem, and all Judaea, and the whole area around the Jordan, were going off to him. ⁶They were being baptized by him in the river Jordan, confessing their sins.

⁷He saw several Pharisees and Sadducees coming to be baptized by him.

'You brood of vipers!' he said to them. 'Who warned you to escape from the coming wrath? ⁸You'd better prove your repentance by bearing the right sort of fruit! ⁹And you needn't start thinking to yourselves, "We have Abraham as our father." Let me tell you, God is quite capable of raising up children for Abraham from these stones! ¹⁰The axe is already taking aim at the root of the tree. Every tree that doesn't produce good fruit is to be cut down and thrown into the fire.'

The road, the water, the fire and the axe. Four powerful symbols set the scene for where the story of Jesus really starts.

Think first of a police motorcade sweeping through a city street. First there appear motorcycles with flashing blue lights.

People scurry to the side of the road as they approach. Everybody knows what's happening: the king has been away a long time, and he's come back at last. Two large black cars come by, filled with bodyguards and officials. Then the car with a flag at the front, containing the king himself. By this time the road is clear; no other cars are in sight; everyone is standing still and watching, waving flags and celebrating.

Now take this scene back 2,000 years, and into the hot, dusty desert. The king has been away a long time, and word goes round that he's coming back at last. But how? There isn't even a road. Well, we'd better get one ready. So off goes the herald, shouting to the peoples of the desert: the king is coming! Make a road for him! Make it good and straight!

That message had echoed through the life of the Jewish people for hundreds of years by the time of **John the Baptist**, ever since it was first uttered in Isaiah 40. It was part of the great message of hope, of forgiveness, of healing for the nation after the horror of **exile**. God would at last come back, bringing comfort and rescue. Yes, John is saying; that's what's happening now. It's time to get ready! The king, God himself, is coming back! Get ready for God's **kingdom**! And John's striking message made everyone sit up and take notice. In today's language, they saw the blue flashing lights, and stopped what they were doing to get ready.

But the trouble was that they *weren't* ready, not by a long way. You may think your house is reasonably tidy and well kept, but if you suddenly get word that the king is coming to visit you may well suddenly want to give it another spring-clean. And the Jewish people, even the devout ones who worshipped regularly in the **Temple**, knew in their bones that they weren't ready for God to come back. The prophets had said that God would come back when the people repented, turning to him with all their hearts. That was what John summoned them to do; and they came in droves.

17

They came for **baptism**. John was plunging them in the water of the river Jordan as they confessed their sins. This wasn't just a symbolic cleansing for individuals; it was a sign of the new thing that God was doing in history, for Israel and the world. Over a thousand years before, the children of Israel had crossed the Jordan when they first entered and conquered the promised land. Now they had to go through the river again, as a sign that they were getting ready for a greater conquest, God's defeat of all evil and the establishment of his kingdom on earth as in **heaven**.

John's message wasn't all comfort. Far from it. He spoke of a fire that would blaze, an axe that would chop down the tree. When he saw some of the Jewish religious leaders, the **Pharisees** and **Sadducees**, coming for baptism, he scoffed at them. They were like snakes slithering away from the bonfire where they'd been hiding, as soon as it started to burn. The only thing that would make John change his mind about them would be if they really behaved differently. Going through the motions of baptism wasn't enough. Real **repentance** meant a complete and lasting change of heart and life. That was the only way to get the road ready for the coming king.

So what were they to repent of? The Pharisees prided themselves on their purity; they were unlikely to be guilty of gross or obvious sins. Yes, but their pride itself was getting in the way of God's homecoming, and their arrogance towards other Israelites, let alone towards the rest of the world, was quite out of keeping with the humility needed before the coming king. We shall see more about that in due course.

In particular, John attacks their confidence in their ancestry. 'We have Abraham as our father,' they would say to themselves. In other words, 'God made promises to Abraham; we are his children; therefore God is committed to us, and we are bound to be all right in the end.' Not so fast, warns John. Your God is the sovereign creator, and it's no trouble to him to create new children for Abraham out of the very stones at your feet. The axe is ready and waiting to chop down the tree; when the king arrives, he will bring judgment as well as mercy, and the only way to avoid it is to show that you are a fruitful tree. (Jesus himself used this image on more than one occasion.) The alternative is the bonfire.

John's stark warnings set the tone for much of the story of Jesus. John prepared the way, not knowing what it would actually look like when God's kingdom arrived; and John was himself puzzled at the outcome (11.2–6). Jesus' own mission was quite different from what people sometimes imagine; the comfort and healing of his kingdom-message was balanced by the stern and solemn warning that when God comes back he demands absolute allegiance. If God really is God, he isn't simply the kindly, indulgent, easy-going parent we sometimes imagine.

The God who came to his people in Jesus will one day unveil his kingdom in all its glory, bringing justice and joy to the whole world. How can we get ready for that day? Where do the roads need straightening out? What fires need to be lit, to burn away the rubbish in his path? Which dead trees will need to be cut down? And, equally important, who should be summoned, right now, to repent?

MATTHEW 3.11–17

Jesus' Baptism

[11]'I am baptizing you with water, for repentance,' John continued. 'But the one who is coming behind me is more powerful than me! I'm not even worthy to carry his sandals. He will baptize you with the Holy Spirit and fire! [12]He's got his shovel in his hand, ready to clear out his barn, and gather all his corn into the granary. But he'll burn up the chaff with a fire that will never go out.'

19

¹³Then Jesus arrived at the Jordan from Galilee, and came to John to be baptized by him.

¹⁴John tried to stop him.

'I ought to be baptized by you,' he said, 'And are you going to come to me?'

¹⁵'This is how it's got to be right now,' said Jesus. 'This is the right way for us to complete God's whole saving plan.'

So John consented, ¹⁶and Jesus was baptized. All at once, as he came up out of the water, suddenly the heavens were opened, and he saw God's spirit coming down like a dove and landing on him.

¹⁷Then there came a voice out of the heavens.

'This is my son, my beloved one,' said the voice. 'I am delighted with him.'

It's safe to say that **John** was as surprised as we are.

Or at least, as we should be if we read this passage without knowing what's coming. To get the flavour, imagine that we are going to a huge concert hall, packed to the doors with eager and excited music-lovers. We all have our programmes in hand, waiting for the thunderous music to begin. We know what it ought to sound like. This will be music for a battle, for a victory, thunder and lightning and explosions of wonderful noise. The concert manager comes on stage and declares in ringing tones that the famous musician has arrived. He gets us all on our feet, to welcome with an ovation the man who is going to fulfil all our expectations.

As we stand there eagerly, a small figure comes on the stage. He doesn't look at all like what we expected. He is carrying, not a conductor's baton, to bring the orchestra to life, but a small flute. As we watch, shocked into silence, he plays, gently and softly, a tune quite different to what we had imagined. But, as we listen, we start to hear familiar themes played in a new way. The music is haunting and fragile, winging its way into our imaginations and hopes and transforming them. And, as it reaches its close, as though at a signal, the orchestra responds with a new version of the music we had been expecting all along.

Now listen to John as the concert manager, whipping us into excitement at the soloist who is going to appear. 'He's coming! He's more powerful than me! He will give you God's wind and God's fire, not just water! He'll sort you out – he'll clear out the mess – he'll clean up God's farm so that only the good wheat is left!' We are on our feet, expecting a great leader, perhaps the living God himself, sweeping into the hall with a great explosion, a blaze of light and colour, transforming everything in a single blow.

And instead we get Jesus. The Jesus we have only met so far, in Matthew's **gospel**, as a baby with a price on his head. A Jesus who comes and stands humbly before John, asking for **baptism**, sharing the penitential mood of the rest of Judaea, Jerusalem and Galilee. A Jesus who seems to be identifying himself, not with a God who sweeps all before him in judgment, but with the people who are themselves facing that judgment and needing to repent.

John, of course, is horrified. He seems to have known that Jesus was the one he was waiting for; but why then would he be coming for baptism? What's happened to the agenda? What's happened to the wind and fire, to the clearing out of God's farm? Surely if anything he, John, needs to be baptized by Jesus himself?

Jesus' reply tells us something vital about the whole gospel story that is going to unfold before our surprised gaze. Yes, he is coming to fulfil God's plan, the promises which God made ages ago and has never forgotten. Yes, these are promises which will blow God's wind, God's **spirit**, through the world, which will bring the fire of God's just judgment on evil wherever it occurs, and which will rescue God's penitent people once and for all from every kind of **exile** to which they have been driven. But if he, Jesus, is to do all this, this is how he

21

must do it: by humbly identifying himself with God's people, by taking their place, sharing their penitence, living their life and ultimately dying their death.

What good will this do? And how will it bring about the result that John – and his audience – were longing for?

To those questions, Matthew's full answer is: read the rest of the story. But we can already glimpse what that answer will be when Jesus comes up out of the water. Israel came through the water of the Red Sea and was given the **law**, confirming their status as God's son, God's firstborn. Jesus came up from the water of baptism and received God's spirit, God's wind, God's breath, in a new way, declaring him to be God's son, Israel-in-person. The dove, though, which for a moment embodies and symbolizes the spirit, indicates that the coming judgment will not be achieved through a warlike or vindictive spirit, but will mean the making of peace. Judgment itself is judged by this spirit, just as Jesus will at last take the judgment upon himself and make an end of it.

Part of the challenge of this passage is to learn afresh to be surprised by Jesus. He comes to fulfil God's plans, not ours, and even his prophets sometimes seem to misunderstand what he's up to. He will not always play the music we expect. But if we learn to listen carefully to what he says, and watch carefully what he does, we will find that our real longings, the hunger beneath the surface excitement, will be richly met.

At the same time, those who in **repentance** and **faith** follow Jesus through baptism and along the road he will now lead us will find, if we listen, that the same voice from **heaven** speaks to us as well. As we learn to put aside our own plans and submit to his, we may be granted moments of vision, glimpses of his greater reality. And at the centre of that sudden sight we will find our loving father, affirming us as his children, equipping us, too, with his spirit so that our lives may be swept clean and made ready for use.

MATTHEW 4.1–11

Temptation in the Wilderness

[1]Then Jesus was led out into the wilderness by the spirit to be tested by the devil. [2]He fasted for forty days and forty nights, and at the end of it was famished. [3]Then the tempter approached him.

'If you really are God's son,' he said, 'tell these stones to become bread!'

[4]'The Bible says,' replied Jesus, 'that people don't live only on bread. We live on every word that comes from God's mouth.'

[5]Then the devil took him off to the holy city, and stood him on a pinnacle of the Temple.

[6]'If you really are God's son,' he said, 'throw yourself down. The Bible does say, after all, that

God will command his angels to look after you,
and they will carry you in their hands,
so that you won't hurt your foot against a stone.'

[7]'But the Bible also says', replied Jesus, 'that you mustn't make the Lord your God prove himself!'

[8]Then the devil took him off again, this time to a very high mountain. There he showed him all the magnificent kingdoms of the world.

[9]'I'll give the whole lot to you,' he said, 'if you will fall down and worship me.'

[10]'Get out of it, satan!' replied Jesus. 'The Bible says, "Worship the Lord your God, and serve him alone!"'

[11]Then the devil left him, and angels came and looked after him.

Jennifer went for a long walk in the woods. It had been an exhausting six months, and she needed time to think.

She had concentrated on the campaign. Ever since her local party had told her, to her surprise, that they wanted her to be their candidate, she had been overwhelmed by the honour both of running for Parliament and of serving her people, her country, the world. All her noble ideals had been smiling at her, beckoning her, telling her that she was now going to be able to achieve them. Her one thought had been: get elected, and at last you'll be able to change the world! To make things better. To turn things around.

Then the last frantic days of the campaign. Touring the area, shaking hands, making speeches, late-night sessions with party workers, snatched sleep, too much coffee, more speeches, more handshakes. And finally the election. She still couldn't believe it. Victory by 10,000 votes. They had wanted *her*. They had chosen *her*. This was her day, and it was sweet.

But she needed space to think, to reflect, to work it all through. Hence the long walk in the woods by herself.

She was shocked at what she discovered. The ideals were still there – the dreams of service, of changing the world. But what were these other voices?

'Now at last,' they whispered, 'you've got a chance to make some real money. Lots of businesses will want you on their board, to lobby ministers for them. You can name your price.'

'This is just the first rung on the ladder,' said the voices. 'If you play your cards well, if you don't make a fuss about too many things, and get to know the right people, you could be a government minister . . . in the Cabinet . . . fame and popularity . . . press conferences, TV appearances . . .'

What was happening? Where were these voices coming from?

But there was more.

'Think what you could do now,' the voices whispered. 'That party activist you've never liked – you could get rid of him. You've got power. And you'll have more. The world is your chessboard. Go ahead and play the game your way!'

One early Christian writer tells us that Jesus was tempted

like other humans in every possible way (Hebrews 4.15). We shouldn't be surprised, then, that after his great moment of vision, when his sense of God's calling and love was so dramatically confirmed at his **baptism**, he had to face the whispering voices and recognize them for what they were. These suggestions are all ways of distorting the true vocation: the vocation to be a truly human being, to be God's person, to be a servant to the world and to other people. Jesus must face these temptations now, and win at least an initial victory over them. If he doesn't, they will meet him suddenly, in the middle of his work, and they may overwhelm him.

The first two temptations play on the very strength he has just received. 'You are my son, my beloved one!', God had said to him. Very well, whispers the demonic voice; if you really are God's son, surely he can't want you to go hungry when you have the power to get food for yourself? Surely you want people to see who you are? Why not do something really spectacular? And then, dropping the apparent logic, the enemy comes out boldly: forget your heavenly father. Just worship me and I'll give you power, greatness like no one else ever had.

Jesus sees through the trap. He answers, each time, with the Bible and with God. He is committed to living off God's **word**; to trusting God completely, without setting up trick tests to put God on the spot. He is committed to loving and serving God alone. The flesh may scream for satisfaction; the world may beckon seductively; the devil himself may offer undreamed-of power; but Israel's loving God, the one Jesus knew as father, offered the reality of what it meant to be human, to be a true Israelite, to be **Messiah**.

The biblical texts Jesus used as his key weapons help us to see how this remarkable story fits into Matthew's **gospel** at this point. They are all taken from the story of Israel in the wilderness. Jesus had come through the waters of baptism, like Israel crossing the Red Sea. He now had to face, in forty days and nights, the equivalent of Israel's forty years in the desert. But, where Israel failed again and again, Jesus succeeded. Here at last is a true Israelite, Matthew is saying. He has come to do what God always wanted Israel to do – to bring light to the world (see verse 16).

Behind that again is the even deeper story of Adam and Eve in the garden. A single command; a single temptation; a single, devastating, result. Jesus kept his eyes on his father, and so launched the mission to undo the age-old effects of human rebellion. He would meet the tempter again in various guises: protesting to him, through his closest associate, that he should change his mind about going to the cross (16.23); mocking him, through the **priests** and bystanders, as he hung on the cross (27.39–43, again with the words 'if you are God's son'). This is no accident. When Jesus refused to go the way of the tempter he was embracing the way of the cross. The enticing whispers that echoed around his head were designed to distract him from his central vocation, the road to which his baptism had committed him, the path of servanthood that would lead to suffering and death. They were meant to stop him from carrying out God's calling, to redeem Israel and the world.

The temptations we all face, day by day and at critical moments of decision and vocation in our lives, may be very different from those of Jesus, but they have exactly the same point. They are not simply trying to entice us into committing this or that sin. They are trying to distract us, to turn us aside, from the path of servanthood to which our baptism has commissioned us. God has a costly but wonderfully glorious vocation for each one of us. The enemy will do everything possible to distract us and thwart God's purpose. If we have heard God's voice welcoming us as his children, we will also hear the whispered suggestions of the enemy.

But, as God's children, we are entitled to use the same defence as the **son of God** himself. Store scripture in your heart, and know how to use it. Keep your eyes on God, and trust him for everything. Remember your calling, to bring God's light into the world. And say a firm 'no' to the voices that lure you back into the darkness.

MATTHEW 4.12–17

Announcing the Kingdom

[12]When Jesus heard that John had been arrested, he went off to Galilee. [13]He left Nazareth, and went to live at Capernaum, a small town by the sea in the region of Zebulon and Naphtali. [14]This happened so that the word spoken through Isaiah the prophet might come true:

> [15]The land of Zebulon and the land of Naphtali,
> The road by the sea, beyond the Jordan,
> Galilee, land of the nations:
> [16]The people who sat in the dark saw a great light;
> Light dawned on those who sat in the shadowy land of death.

[17]From that time on Jesus began to make his proclamation. 'Repent!' he would say. 'The kingdom of heaven is arriving!'

I once knew a small boy (no, it wasn't me, actually) who used to telephone people at random. When a voice answered the phone, he would say, 'Are you on the line?' 'Yes,' the unsuspecting victim would reply. 'Well, get off quick!' he would shout. 'There's a train coming!'

The warning of an approaching object or event is always important. We need to know what's coming, what danger it poses, what action we should take. And in the case of Jesus, and of the way Matthew tells us about him, there is one thing supremely important: we need to know what this **kingdom of heaven** is that he said was approaching, and what action he expected people to take. Though this is central to everything

Jesus was and did, and to everything that the **gospels** say about him, it is remarkable how few people really grasp what was going on.

First things first. Matthew normally has Jesus speak of the 'kingdom of heaven'; the other gospels normally use the phrase 'kingdom of God'. Saying 'heaven' instead of 'God' was a regular Jewish way of avoiding the word 'God' out of reverence and respect. We must clear out of our minds any thought that 'kingdom of heaven' means a place, namely '**heaven**', seen as the place where God's people go after their death. That, after all, would make no sense here. How could this sort of kingdom be said to be 'approaching' or 'arriving'?

No. If 'kingdom of heaven' means the same as 'kingdom of God', then we have a much clearer idea of what Jesus had in mind. Anyone who was warning people about something that was about to happen must have known that the people he was talking to would understand. And any first-century Jew, hearing someone talking about God's kingdom, or the kingdom of heaven, would know. This meant revolution.

Jesus grew up in the shadow of kingdom-movements. The Romans had conquered his homeland about sixty years before he was born. They were the last in a long line of pagan nations to do so. They had installed Herod the Great, and then his sons after him, as puppet monarchs to do their dirty work for them. Most Jews resented both parts of this arrangement, and longed for a chance to revolt.

But they weren't just eager for freedom in the way that most subject peoples are. They wanted it because of what they believed about God, themselves and the world. If there was one God who had made the whole world, and if they were his special people, then it couldn't be God's will to have pagan foreigners ruling them. What's more, God had made promises in their scriptures that one day he would indeed rescue them and put everything right. And these promises focused on one thing in particular: God would become king. King not only of Israel but of the whole world. A king who would bring justice and peace at last, who would turn the upside-down world the right way up again. There should be no king but God, the revolutionaries believed. God's kingdom, the kingdom of heaven, was what they longed for, prayed for, worked for, and were prepared to die for.

And now Jesus was declaring that God's kingdom, the sovereign rule of heaven, was approaching like an express train. Those who were standing idly by had better take note and get out of the way. God's kingdom meant danger as well as hope. If justice and peace are on the way, those who have twisted justice or disturbed peace may be in trouble. They had better get their act together while there's time. And the good old word for that is: 'Repent!'

The trouble with that word, too, is that people have often not understood it. They have thought it means 'feeling bad about yourself'. It doesn't. It means 'change direction'; 'turn round and go the other way;' or 'stop what you're doing and do the opposite instead'. How you *feel* about it isn't the really important thing. It's what you *do* that matters.

Jesus believed that his contemporaries were going in the wrong direction. They were bent on revolution of the standard kind: military resistance to occupying forces, leading to a takeover of power. Part of the underlying theme of his temptations in the wilderness was the suggestion that he should use his own status, as God's **Messiah**, to launch some kind of movement that would sweep him to power, privilege and glory.

The problem with all these movements was that they were fighting darkness with darkness, and Israel was called – and Jesus was called – to bring God's *light* into the world. That's why Matthew hooks up Jesus' early preaching with the prophecy of Isaiah that spoke about people in the dark being dazzled by sudden light, a prophecy which went on to speak about the child to be born, the coming Messiah, through whom God would truly liberate Israel at last (Isaiah 9.1–7). Jesus could see that the standard kind of revolution, fighting and killing in order to put an end to . . . fighting and killing, was a nonsense. Doing it in God's name was a blasphemous nonsense.

But the trouble was that many of his contemporaries were eager to get on with the fight. His message of **repentance** was not, therefore, that they should feel sorry for personal and private sins (though he would of course want that as well), but that as a nation they should stop rushing towards the cliff edge of violent revolution, and instead go the other way, towards God's kingdom of light and peace and healing and forgiveness, for themselves and for the world.

What would happen if they didn't? Gradually, as Matthew's story develops, we begin to realize. If the light-bearers insist on darkness, darkness they shall have. If the peace-people insist on war, war they shall have. If the people called to bring God's love and forgiveness into the world insist on hating everyone else, hatred and all that it brings will come crashing around their ears. This won't be an arbitrary judgment or punishment; it will be what they themselves have been calling for. This is why they must repent while there's still time. The kingdom is coming, and they are standing in the way.

The message is just as urgent today, if not more so for us who live on this side of Calvary and Easter. Matthew would want to say to us that the kingdom which Jesus established through his own work, and his death and **resurrection**, now faces us with the same challenge. Are we working to extend God's kingdom in the world? Or are we standing in its way?

MATTHEW 4.18–25

Jesus Calls the Disciples

¹⁸As Jesus was walking beside the Sea of Galilee he saw two

brothers, Simon (also called Peter) and Andrew his brother. They were fishermen, and were casting nets into the sea.

[19] 'Follow me!' said Jesus. 'I'll make you fish for people!'

[20] Straight away they abandoned their nets and followed him.

[21] He went on further, and saw two other brothers, James the son of Zebedee and John his brother. They were in the boat, mending their nets, with Zebedee their father. He called them. [22] At once they left the boat, and their father, and followed him.

[23] He went on through the whole of Galilee, teaching in their synagogues and proclaiming the good news of the kingdom, healing every disease and every illness among the people.

[24] Word about him went out around the whole of Syria. They brought to him all the people tormented with various kinds of diseases and ailments, demon-possessed people, epileptics, and paralytics, and he healed them. [25] Large crowds followed him from Galilee, the Decapolis, Jerusalem, Judaea and beyond the Jordan.

If you go to Galilee today they will show you a boat that might have belonged to Andrew and Peter, or perhaps the Zebedee family.

In one of the most remarkable archaeological finds anywhere in the Holy Land (which is full of them), a boat was found sticking out of the mud one summer when the level of the Sea of Galilee dropped dramatically in a period of dry weather. With great care it was lifted clear of the sea bottom, cleaned and preserved. Now, in a special exhibit, millions of visitors can see the sort of boat Jesus' first followers used for fishing. It has been carbon-dated to exactly the period of Jesus' life.

The boat is a vivid reminder of the day-to-day existence of his followers – and of what it cost them to give it all up and follow Jesus. They were, in today's language, small business-men, working as families not for huge profits but to make enough to live on and have a little over. Fish were plentiful and there were good markets. In a cosmopolitan area, with soldiers, wayfarers, pilgrims and pedlars coming and going, as well as the local population, people would always want what they were selling. But it was hard work, and sometimes dangerous. Their lives were modestly secure, but hardly luxurious.

So why did they give it all up to follow a wandering preacher?

The same question faces people today. Why did this person give up a promising legal career to become a preacher, throwing away a lifetime of high earnings for the insecurity and poverty of pastoring and teaching a church? Why did that person abandon her remarkable gifts as a singer in order to study theology and get ordained? Why did this person become a teacher, that one a prison governor, this one a monk, that one a missionary? And – since these more obvious callings are only the tip of the iceberg of Christian vocation – why do Christians in millions of other walks of life regularly give up lifestyles and practices that look attractive and lucrative in order to maintain honesty, integrity, **faith**, hope and love?

The answer can only be in Jesus himself, and in the astonishing magnetism of his presence and personality. This can be known and felt today, as we meditate on the stories about him and pray to know him better, just as the first **disciples** knew and felt his presence 2,000 years ago. Sometimes his call comes slowly, starting like a faint murmur and growing until we can no longer ignore it. Sometimes he calls people as suddenly and dramatically as he called Peter and Andrew, James and John. When that happens to you, by whatever means and at whatever pace, you will know; Jesus has a way of getting through, and whatever we are engaged with – whatever nets we are mending, or fish we are catching – somehow we will be sufficiently aware of his presence and call to know what it is we're being asked to do.

At least, we will know we're being asked to follow him. We won't necessarily know where it's all going to lead, and we wouldn't perhaps be quite so eager if we did. 'You'll be catching people now!' was what Jesus said to Peter and Andrew; what did they think that would mean? Did they know how the 'people' in question would feel about it? Did they have any inkling that both of them would end up being crucified, as their master would be? Did James, the brother of John, have the slightest idea that within a few years he would be dead, killed on the orders of Herod?

No, they didn't. God in his mercy reveals things little by little. Nor did Peter think that he would end up with a huge church in Rome dedicated to his memory; or Andrew suppose that whole countries (Scotland, Greece, Russia) would regard him as their patron saint. They saw neither the glory nor the pain, that day when a young man walked by the sea in their little town of Capernaum, on the north shore of the Sea of Galilee. They only saw him; and that was enough. In him, as Paul might have said, all the treasures of glory and pain are hidden. That is what the **gospel** story is all about.

But it wasn't just personal magnetism that drew people from hundreds of miles around to seek out this Jesus as he went to and fro across the region of Galilee. It was his remark-able healings. Matthew will tell us more stories about such events in due course. For the moment, in quick summary fashion, he tells us how word suddenly went out that people whose lives had been blighted by every kind of illness and disease – and we only have to think for a minute of life before modern medicine to realize what that would mean – could be healed if they came to this extraordinary man.

Historians today are agreed that this is the only explanation for the crowds Jesus drew. He really did have remarkable powers of healing. But Jesus was never simply a healer pure and simple, vital though that was as part of his work. For him, the healings were signs of the new thing that God was doing through him. God's **kingdom** – God's sovereign, saving rule –

was at last being unleashed upon Israel and the world, through him. How could this not bring healing in its wake? Soon the fishermen found themselves, not placidly working at their family craft beside the lake, but at the centre of bustling crowds. Jesus' mission was well and truly launched, and they were caught up in it.

What pulls in the crowds today? Entertainment, of course: football, rock music, big fireworks parties. Great national tragedies, such as the death of a popular princess, or a major disaster. What would it take – what could and should Jesus' followers be doing today – that would send people off with the word that something new was happening and that everyone should come quickly?

MATTHEW 5.1–12

The Beatitudes

[1]When Jesus saw the crowds, he went up the hillside, and sat down. His disciples came to him. [2]He took a deep breath, and began his teaching:

[3]'Wonderful news for the poor in spirit! The kingdom of heaven is yours.

[4]'Wonderful news for the mourners! You're going to be comforted.

[5]'Wonderful news for the meek! You're going to inherit the earth.

[6]'Wonderful news for people who hunger and thirst for God's justice! You're going to be satisfied.

[7]'Wonderful news for the merciful! You'll receive mercy yourselves.

[8]'Wonderful news for the pure in heart! You will see God.

[9]'Wonderful news for the peacemakers! You'll be called God's children.

[10]'Wonderful news for people who are persecuted because of God's way! The kingdom of heaven belongs to you.

¹¹'Wonderful news for you, when people slander you and persecute you, and say all kinds of wicked things about you falsely because of me! ¹²Celebrate and rejoice: there's a great reward for you in heaven. That's how they persecuted the prophets who went before you.'

Many years ago there was a dramatic movie about the first test pilots to break the sound barrier. No plane had ever flown faster than the speed of sound. Many people didn't believe it was possible. Some thought the plane would disintegrate under the forces that would be generated. Eventually, in the movie, various pilots took their planes over the magic figure of 735 miles per hour, only to have the planes disintegrate with the huge vibrations, or to crash. The controls, it seemed, refused to work properly once the plane came to the sound barrier.

Finally, at the climax of the movie, another test pilot figured out what to do. It seemed that when the plane broke the sound barrier *the controls began to work backwards*. Pulling the stick to make the plane bring its nose up sent it downwards instead. Greatly daring, he flew to the same speed. At the critical moment, instead of pulling the stick back, he pushed it forwards. That would normally send the plane into a dive, but his hunch had been correct. The nose came up, and the plane flew on, fast and free, faster than anyone had travelled before.

The story is not historically accurate. Chuck Yeager, the first human to move faster than the speed of sound in real life, was often asked whether he'd done it the way it was shown in the movie, but he insisted it wasn't like that. However, the story gives a graphic illustration of what Jesus is doing in these apparently simple words. He is taking the controls and making them work backwards.

The only explanation seems to be that he thinks he is taking God's people through the sound barrier – taking them somewhere they'd never been before. The one thing most people know about planes going through the sound barrier is that you hear a loud explosion. Many of Jesus' contemporaries would have said that this was a good picture of the effect he had.

Jesus wasn't simply a great teacher, and if we try to describe him like that we will misunderstand him. This passage is the beginning of the famous 'Sermon on the Mount', which runs through chapters 5, 6 and 7 of Matthew's **gospel**, and sets out, in Matthew's presentation of it, the main themes of Jesus' proclamation. People often say what wonderful teaching the Sermon on the Mount is, and that if only people would obey it the world would be a better place. But if we think of Jesus simply sitting there telling people how to behave properly, we will miss what was really going on. These 'blessings', the 'wonderful news' that he's announcing, are not saying 'try hard to live like this.' They are saying that people who already *are* like that are in good shape. They should be happy and celebrate.

Jesus is not suggesting that these are simply timeless truths about the way the world is, about human behaviour. If he was saying that, he was wrong. Mourners often go uncomforted, the meek don't inherit the earth, those who long for justice frequently take that longing to the grave. This is an upside-down world, or perhaps a right-way-up world; *and Jesus is saying that with his work it's starting to come true.* This is an announcement, not a philosophical analysis of the world. It's about something that's starting to happen, not about a general truth of life. It is *gospel*: good news, not good advice.

Follow me, Jesus said to the first **disciples**; because in him the living God was doing a new thing, and this list of 'wonderful news' is part of his invitation, part of his summons, part of his way of saying that God is at work in a fresh way and that this is what it looks like. Jesus is beginning a new era for God's people and God's world. From here on, all the controls people thought they knew about are going to work the other way round. In our world, still, most people think that wonderful news consists of success, wealth, long life, victory in battle. Jesus is offering wonderful news for the humble, the poor, the mourners, the peacemakers.

The word for 'wonderful news' is often translated 'blessed', and part of the point is that this is *God's* wonderful news. God is acting in and through Jesus to turn the world upside down, to turn Israel upside down, to pour out lavish 'blessings' on all who now turn to him and accept the new thing that he is doing. (This list is sometimes called 'the Beatitudes', because the Latin word 'beatus' means 'blessed'.) But the point is not to offer a list of what sort of people God normally blesses. The point is to announce God's new **covenant**.

In Deuteronomy, the people came through the wilderness and arrived at the border of the promised land, and God gave them a solemn covenant. He listed the blessings and the curses that would come upon them if they were obedient or disobedient (chapter 28). Now Matthew has shown us Jesus, coming out of Egypt (2.15), through the water and the wilderness (chapters 3 and 4), and into the land of promise (4.12–25). Here, now, is his new covenant.

So when do these promises come true? There is a great temptation for Christians to answer: in **heaven**, after death. At first sight, verses 3, 10 and 11 seem to say this: '**the kingdom of heaven**' belongs to the poor in **spirit** and the persecuted, and there's a great reward 'in heaven' for those who suffer persecution for Jesus' sake. This, though, is a misunderstanding of the meaning of 'heaven'. Heaven is God's space, where full reality exists, close by our ordinary ('earthly') reality and interlocking with it. One day heaven and earth will be joined together for ever, and the true state of affairs, at present out of sight, will be unveiled. After all, verse 5 says that the meek will inherit the earth, and that can hardly happen in a disembodied heaven after death.

No: the clue comes in the next chapter, in the prayer Jesus

taught his followers. We are to pray that God's kingdom will come, and God's will be done, 'on earth as it is in heaven'. The life of heaven – the life of the realm where God is already king – is to become the life of the world, transforming the present 'earth' into the place of beauty and delight that God always intended. *And those who follow Jesus are to begin to live by this rule here and now.* That's the point of the Sermon on the Mount, and these 'beatitudes' in particular. They are a summons to live in the present in the way that will make sense in God's promised future; because that future has arrived in the present in Jesus of Nazareth. It may seem upside down, but we are called to believe, with great daring, that it is in fact the right way up. Try it and see.

MATTHEW 5.13–20

Fulfilling the Law

¹³'You're the salt of the earth! But if the salt becomes tasteless, how is it going to get salty again? It's no good for anything. You might as well throw it out and walk all over it.

¹⁴'You're the light of the world! A city can't be hidden if it's on top of a hill. ¹⁵People don't light a lamp and put it under a bucket; they put it on a lampstand. Then it gives light to every-body in the house. ¹⁶That's how you must shine your light in front of people! Then they will see what wonderful things you do, and they'll give glory to your father in heaven.

¹⁷'Don't suppose that I came to destroy the law and the prophets. I didn't come to destroy them; I came to fulfil them! ¹⁸I'm telling you the truth: until heaven and earth disappear, not one stroke, not one dot, is going to disappear from the law, until it's all come true. ¹⁹So anyone who relaxes a single one of these commandments, even the little ones, and teaches that to people, will be called least in the kingdom of heaven. But anyone who does them and teaches them will be called great in the kingdom of heaven.

20'Yes, let me tell you: unless your covenant behaviour is far superior to that of the scribes and Pharisees, you will never get in to the kingdom of heaven.'

We all know what happens when a revolutionary party suddenly finds itself in power. It's one thing to shout angrily from the sidelines, but quite another to form a government and run a country. All sorts of things have to be organized and dealt with which a rebel movement can happily ignore.

When this happens, two questions are asked. First, can this movement really do the basic things that a government can do better than its predecessor? Was it just making a lot of noise which now turns out to be hot air, or can it really deliver the goods? Second, can it remain true to itself and its original ideals even though it's now in power? Will it, in turn, become corrupt and just like all other governments, starting off in a blaze of glory and good intentions and ending up riddled with corruption and muddle?

Jesus was starting a revolution all right – but it was a different sort of revolution from all the other ones that were bubbling up in his days. And he had to do two things at the same time. First, he had to show the Jews of his day that this movement really was the fulfilment of all that Israel had believed and longed for. Second, he had to show that he and his followers really were living by (and also dying by) the new way he was announcing. The tension between these two sometimes seemed fierce, and to this day many people misunderstand it. Some think of Jesus as just a great Jewish teacher without much of a revolution. Others see him as so revolutionary that he left Judaism behind altogether and established something quite new.

This passage shows how Jesus himself held the two together. He was indeed offering something utterly revolutionary, to which he would remain faithful; but it was, in fact, the reality towards which Israel's whole life and tradition had pointed.

This passage, following the striking introduction to the Sermon on the Mount in verses 3–12, introduces the main theme that will occupy Jesus in what follows. He has come to fulfil the **law** and the prophets. Most of the rest of the Sermon explains exactly what that means, right through to 7.11; then 7.12, echoing 5.17, sums it all up. Do to others, he says, what you would like them to do to you, because this is what the law and the prophets are really all about. The Sermon then concludes with sharp warnings about the urgent need to pay attention to what Jesus is saying (7.13–27).

Our present passage, then, is a kind of gateway to all that will follow, and its theme is clear. Jesus is calling the Israel of his day to *be* Israel indeed, now that he is there. What he says here can now be applied to all Christians, but its original meaning was a challenge to Jesus' own contemporaries. God had called Israel to be the salt of the earth; but Israel was behaving like everyone else, with its power politics, its factional squabbles, its militant revolutions. How could God keep the world from going bad – the main function of salt in the ancient world – if Israel, his chosen 'salt', had lost its distinctive taste?

In the same way, God called Israel to be the light of the world (e.g. Isaiah 42.6; 49.6). Israel was the people through whom God intended to shine his bright light into the world's dark corners, not simply to show up evil but to enable people who were blundering around in the dark to find their way. But what if the people called to be the light-bearers had become part of the darkness? That was Jesus' warning – and also his challenge. Jerusalem, the city set on a hill, was supposed to be a beacon of hope to the world. His followers were to be like that: their deep, heartfelt keeping of God's laws would be a sign to the nations around that the one God, the creator, the God of Israel, was God indeed, and that they should worship him.

We can imagine people saying to themselves, 'Well, here's another new teacher who thinks he's got the answer! We've already got teachers of the law; we've already got the **Pharisees** who think their interpretation is the proper one. What's different about this man?'

Jesus gives his answer, straight from the shoulder. The **scribes** and the Pharisees do indeed teach a way of being faithful to God, a way of behaving in accordance with God's **covenant**. But God's own sovereign rule, the '**kingdom of heaven**', is even now breaking in; and those who want to belong to the new world he is opening up must discover a way of covenant behaviour that goes far, far beyond anything the scribes and Pharisees ever dreamed of.

Jesus wasn't intending to abandon the law and the prophets. Israel's whole story, commands, promises and all, was going to come true in him. But, now that he was here, a way was opening up for Israel – and, through that, all the world – to make God's covenant a reality in their own selves, changing behaviour not just by teaching but by a change of heart and mind itself.

This was truly revolutionary, and at the same time deeply in tune with the ancient stories and promises of the Bible. And the remarkable thing is that Jesus brought it all into reality in his own person. He was the salt of the earth. He was the light of the world: set up on a hill-top, crucified for all the world to see, becoming a beacon of hope and new **life** for everybody, drawing people to worship his father, embodying the way of self-giving love which is the deepest fulfilment of the law and the prophets.

That's why these sayings, originally applied to Israel, now apply to all those who follow Jesus and draw on his life as the source of their own. How does this challenge affect us today? Where does the world need salt and light right now, and how can we, through following Jesus, provide it?

MATTHEW 5.21–26

On Murder and Reconciliation

[21]'You heard that it was said to the ancient people, "You shall not murder"; and anyone who commits murder shall be liable to judgment. [22]But I say to you that everyone who is angry with his brother shall be liable to judgment; anyone who uses foul and abusive language will be liable to the lawcourt; and anyone who says, "You fool", will be liable to the fires of Gehenna.

[23]'So, if you are coming to the altar with your gift, and there you remember that your brother has a grievance against you, [24]leave your gift right there in front of the altar, and go first and be reconciled to your brother. Then come back and offer your gift. [25]Make friends with your opponent quickly, while you are with him in the street, in case your opponent hands you over to the judge, and the judge to the officer, and you find yourself being thrown into jail. [26]I'm telling you the truth: you won't get out until you've paid the last penny.'

It happened again the other day. It is sadly common. A leading politician makes a gesture of contempt towards the opposition. Someone on the other side reacts angrily. Soon dozens of people are on their feet, shouting. Insults fly to and fro. Out on the street, supporters of the rival parties jeer at each other, then begin to jostle and threaten. Fists starts to fly. Knives come out. By the time the police arrive two people have been killed. The other side vows revenge. The next day they're back in force, and attack two innocent passers-by. Their families in turn swear to get even. Is this what human life was meant to be like?

Jesus knew this world, too. People of his day who wrote about that world describe incidents just like this. Romans insulting Jews, Samaritans attacking Jews, Jews fighting back, different Jewish parties insulting and attacking each other.

The fault lines often ran through villages, through families, and sometimes even through households. When people are insecure – and during a military occupation both the occupied and the occupiers often feel themselves to be very insecure – they become jumpy, and react badly to anything that even looks like aggression. Often the only thing that prevents all-out war is exhaustion and poverty.

Part of the tragedy of all this is that people take their public anger back into the home. We know this ourselves. The executive whose boss has shouted at him goes back to his own office and shouts at the secretary. The secretary goes home and shouts at the children. The children shout at the cat. If part of human maturity is learning how to recognize your anger, and deal with it before it gets out of control, we have to conclude that most of us are not very mature.

If Israel is called to be the light of the world, and Jesus has come to call Israel back to its true vocation, how can all this be dealt with? How can anger be defused, and prevented from spilling out into violence?

In this section of the Sermon on the Mount, Jesus takes the commands of the **law** and shows how they provide a blueprint for a way of being fully, genuinely, gloriously human. This new way, which Jesus had come to pioneer and make possible, goes deep down into the roots of personality and produces a different pattern of behaviour altogether.

It begins with smouldering anger against someone very close to you. All right, it may not result in murder; but the point of the commandment against murder was not that you should stop short of killing someone, but that you should never get near even the thought that you wish they were dead. What 'judgment' will you incur (verse 22)? God's judgment, clearly; but this isn't simply an arbitrary punishment that will catch up with you eventually, but rather a judgment that will begin right now. Every time you decide to let your anger smoulder on inside you, you are becoming a little less than fully human. You are deciding to belittle yourself. Of course, if you let your anger turn into foul and abusive language, sooner or later you may find yourself in court. And if you are the sort of person who sneers at everybody and calls them names, the fire inside you may eventually become all that's left of you, as **Gehenna** – the smouldering garbage dump of ancient Jerusalem – may take you over completely.

What's the alternative? Jesus offers two remarkably specific and practical commands. Be reconciled; make friends. How simple that is – and yet how hugely difficult and costly! It will almost certainly involve climbing down from the high pedestal on which you have placed yourself, abandoning your position of superiority over the person you're angry with. But genuine humans don't live on pedestals; they have their feet on the ground, on a level with everybody else.

In particular – and this is very striking – reconciliation takes precedence even over worship. Jesus imagines someone getting all the way into the **Temple** courtyard, buying a sacrificial animal on the way, and suddenly remembering (as well one might, when approaching the presence of the loving and holy God) some relationship that has gone wrong. The scene then becomes almost comic. It takes about three days to get back to Galilee, where most of Jesus' hearers lived. He cannot seriously have imagined an anxious worshipper leaving a live animal sitting there in the Temple courts for a week while they scurried back home, apologized to the offended person, and then returned to Jerusalem. As so often in his teaching, he seems to be exaggerating to make the point. The point is that you must live, day by day, in such a way that when you come to worship there is no anger between you and your neighbour, your sister, your brother. Impossible? Jesus implies that it isn't, now that he is here to show the way.

Then the picture widens. You and a neighbour are actually

going before a judge to fight out your legal differences. Don't even get to court, he says. Sort it out beforehand, or you may end up in jail and paying every penny you have. This may well be good advice as it stands, but it most likely reaches far beyond mere lawsuits. Israel in Jesus' day was in trouble, oppressed by pagans from outside and by rich aristocrats from inside. Many Jews longed for their day in God's court when they would be proved right and their enemies overthrown. Don't even think of it like that, says Jesus. Make friends, not enemies. He will return to this point later in the chapter (verses 38–48). Otherwise, what will happen? Your enemies may win after all, and then what will you do?

By the end of the Sermon this coded warning becomes even more explicit. The house will fall with a great crash. Jesus, it seems, is not simply talking about individual anger and behaviour, vital though that is. He is alluding to a yet greater danger. Unless Israel learns, right now, how to be God's chosen people, how to shed God's light into the world, disaster is in store: a disaster which has its roots in personal failure to deal with anger, and its fruits in the national insistence on letting centuries of persecution justify violence.

All this is, of course, impossible. That is, it's impossible until you look at Jesus. As we continue through Matthew's story, we discover that our natural question ('How can people possibly do what he says?') is eventually answered. Jesus himself refused to go the way of anger. Instead, he took the anger of his enemies within Israel, and of Israel's own enemies, the Romans, on to himself, and died under its load. From that point on, reconciliation is not simply an ideal we might strive for. It is an achievement, an accomplishment, which we in turn must now embody.

MATTHEW 5.27–37

On Adultery and Oaths

27'You heard', Jesus continued, 'that it was said, "You shall not commit adultery." 28But I say to you: everyone who gazes at a woman in order to lust after her has already committed adultery with her in his heart. 29If your right eye trips you up, tear it out and throw it away. Yes: it's better for you to have one part of your body destroyed than for the whole body to be thrown into Gehenna. 30And if your right hand trips you up, cut it off and throw it away. Yes: it's better for you to have one part of your body destroyed than for your whole body to go into Gehenna.

31'It was also said, "If someone divorces his wife, he should give her a legal document to prove it." 32But I say to you: everyone who divorces his wife, unless it's in connection with immorality, makes her commit adultery; and anyone who marries a divorced woman commits adultery.

33'Again, you heard that it was said to the people long ago: "You shall not swear falsely, but you shall give to the Lord what you promised under oath." 34But I say to you: don't swear at all! Don't swear by heaven (it's God's throne!); 35don't swear by the earth (it's God's footstool!); don't swear by Jerusalem (it's the city of the great king!); 36don't swear by your head (you can't make one hair of it turn white or black!). 37When you're talking, say "Yes" when you mean Yes, and "No" when you mean No. Anything more than that comes from the evil one.'

As I was getting ready to write this section, an email arrived from an old friend in another country. His church, he said, was facing a question that troubles a great many churches in our day. What did Jesus really mean in his teaching about divorce? I decided to write this section first, thinking the question through as I did so, and then reply.

Clearly, this is a painful and pressing issue for many people around the world. Almost any large congregation these days will have at least some divorced people among its members. Many will have couples who have remarried after divorce. Not many years ago most clergy were unable, in conscience, to give Holy Communion to such people; yet now most churches, of whatever sort and in most parts of the world, receive remarried couples as full members, even if they continue to regard divorce as a great evil. Indeed, many clergy themselves, in many Christian denominations, have been through divorce and remarriage. As I write, I think not only of today's correspondent, but of some very close friends, and some members of my own family, who are in this situation. What must we say? What did Jesus mean? How practical is his teaching today?

This passage is not, of course, the only place in the New Testament where the matter comes up. It is important to study Mark 10.2–12, Luke 16.18, and 1 Corinthians 7.10–16, as well as the present passage and Matthew 19.3–9. Together they show both that Jesus set his face firmly against divorce (in line with Old Testament teaching, e.g. Malachi 2.14–16) and that the early church wrestled with how to apply this in practice.

It is also important to notice that in the present passage the mention of divorce comes between two other issues, both of which are in some ways more basic. It may be stating the obvious to point out that if people knew how to control their bodily lusts on the one hand (verses 27–30), and were committed to complete integrity and truth-telling on the other (verses 33–37), there would be fewer, if any, divorces. Divorce normally happens when lust and lies have been allowed to grow up like weeds and choke the fragile and beautiful plant of marriage.

The first answer, then, is clear. Deal ruthlessly with the first signs of lust. Plucking out eyes and cutting off hands are deliberate exaggerations (like leaving an animal for a week at the altar while you go off to be reconciled), but they make the point very forcibly. Don't suppose that Jesus means you must never feel the impulse of lust when you look at someone attractive. That would be impossible, and is not in any case what the words mean. What he commands us to avoid is the gaze, and the lustful imagination, that follow the initial impulse. Likewise, determine resolutely to tell the truth, to yourself and to your spouse. These two between them will see off most of the challenges that even a hard-pressed modern marriage will face. If the church had carefully taught these disciplines over the years we would have less of a problem now.

But we must start where we are, not where we are not, as Matthew and Paul both clearly recognize. For Matthew, here and in chapter 19, sexual immorality by one partner – presumably an adulterous relationship of some kind – is sufficient grounds for divorce. For Paul, if a Christian is married to a non-Christian, and the non-Christian wants to separate, that too is sufficient; though he insists, despite what some in his churches may well have felt and wanted, that the Christian should not initiate the split. And it seems clear to me (though not to all writers on this subject) that in both of these cases divorce is only divorce if it allows for remarriage. To put that the other way round: if one is not allowed to remarry, then divorce has not really taken place. So if in these two cases divorce is clearly allowed, we must assume that remarriage is at least potentially envisaged.

Perhaps the most important thing to say here, though, is that Jesus certainly didn't want his hearers, or the later church, to get embroiled in endless debates about what precisely was allowed. Far, far more important to think about how to be the light of the world, the salt of the earth! And in the area of sexual behaviour, the answer is clear, bracing and just as challenging today as it was to the wider pagan world of the first century. Sexual desire, though itself good and God-given, is like the fire of **Gehenna**, which needs firmly keeping in place. Saying 'no' to desire when it strikes inappropriately – in other words, outside the context of marriage – is part of the most basic Christian discipline.

This is not 'repression', as people sometimes suggest. It is more like the pruning of a rose, cutting off some healthy buds so that the plant may grow stronger and produce better flowers. Choosing not to be swept along by inappropriate sexual passion may well feel on occasion like cutting off a hand or plucking out an eye, and our world has frequently tried to tell us that doing this is very bad for us. But, for neither the first nor the last time, we must choose to obey our Lord rather than the world.

Jesus' comments about speech and swearing appear to be a deepening of the second commandment, not to take the Lord's name in vain. Most things people regularly swore by in the casual speech of his day could be traced back to God. Better think before you speak, mean what you say, and learn the lesson that, in speaking, less is often more. Extra words, especially 'strong' ones, call into question the speaker's basic truthfulness. If you need to add them, maybe we can't trust you at all.

Throughout this chapter, Jesus is not just giving moral commands. He is unveiling a whole new way of being human. No wonder it looks strange. But Jesus himself pioneered it, and invites us to follow.

MATTHEW 5.38–48

Loving Your Enemies

[38]'You heard that it was said, "An eye for an eye, and a tooth for a tooth." [39]But I say to you: don't use violence to resist evil! Instead, when someone hits you on the right cheek, turn the other one towards him. [40]When someone wants to sue you and

take your shirt, let him have your cloak, too. [41]And when someone forces you to go one mile, go a second one with him. [42]Give to anyone who asks you, and don't refuse someone who wants to borrow from you.

[43]'You heard that it was said, "Love your neighbour and hate your enemy." [44]But I tell you: love your enemies! Pray for people who persecute you! [45]That way, you'll be children of your father in heaven! After all, he makes his sun rise on bad and good alike, and sends rain both on the upright and on the unjust. [46]Look at it like this: if you love those who love you, do you expect a special reward? Even tax-collectors do that, don't they? [47]And if you only greet your own family, what's so special about that? Even Gentiles do that, don't they? [48]Well then: you must be perfect, just as your heavenly father is perfect.'

There was once a father who had to go away from his young family for three or four days on business. Anxious that his wife should be properly looked after in his absence, he had a word with the oldest son, who was nine at the time.

'When I'm away,' he said, 'I want you to think what I would normally do around the house, and you do it for me.' He had in mind, of course, clearing up in the kitchen, washing up dishes, putting out the garbage, and similar tasks.

On his return, he asked his wife what the son had done. 'Well,' she said, 'it was very strange. Straight after breakfast he made himself another cup of coffee, went into the living room, put on some loud music, and read the newspaper for half an hour.' The father was left wondering whether his son had obeyed him a bit too accurately.

The shocking thing about this passage in the Sermon on the Mount is that we are told to watch what our heavenly father is doing and then do the same ourselves. Here is the puzzle: Israel, the chosen people, are challenged to realize that God doesn't have favourites! What sense can we make of that? If they are chosen, doesn't that mean they are God's favourites?

The answer to the puzzle is found earlier in the Sermon. Israel isn't chosen in order to be God's special people while the rest of the world remains in outer darkness. Israel is chosen to be the light of the world, the salt of the earth. Israel is chosen so that, through Israel, God can bless all people. And now Jesus is calling Israel to *be* the light of the world at last. He is opening the way, carving a path through the jungle towards that vocation, urging his followers to come with him on the dangerous road.

And dangerous it is. Not only has Israel in Jesus' day got many enemies, pagan nations who have overrun the land and made the people subject to harsh rules and taxes. There are just as many dangers within, as movements of national resistance spring up, fuelled by anger at the increasing injustice and wickedness. And, within that again, the divisions within Jewish society are becoming more marked, with a few becoming very rich and the majority being poor, some very poor.

These were all pressing issues for the people listening to Jesus. How did his **kingdom**-message apply to them? How can it then apply to us today?

Jesus offers *a new sort of justice*, a creative, healing, restorative justice. The old justice found in the Bible was designed to prevent revenge running away with itself. Better an eye for an eye and a tooth for a tooth than an escalating feud with each side going one worse than the other. But Jesus goes one better still. Better to have no vengeance at all, but rather a creative way forward, reflecting the astonishingly patient love of God himself, who wants Israel to shine his light into the world so that all people will see that he is the one true God, and that his deepest nature is overflowing love. No other god encourages people to behave in a way like this!

So Jesus gives three hints of the sort of thing he has in mind. To be struck on the right cheek, in that world, almost certainly meant being hit with the back of the right hand.

That's not just violence, but an insult: it implies that you're an inferior, perhaps a slave, a child, or (in that world, and sometimes even today) a woman. What's the answer? Hitting back only keeps the evil in circulation. Offering the other cheek implies: hit me again if you like, but now as an equal, not an inferior.

Or suppose you're in a lawcourt where a powerful enemy is suing you (perhaps for non-payment of some huge debt) and wants the shirt off your back. You can't win; but you can show him what he's really doing. Give him your cloak as well; and, in a world where most people only wore those two garments, shame him with your impoverished nakedness. This is what the rich, powerful and careless are doing. They are reducing the poor to a state of shame.

The third example clearly reflects the Roman military occupation. Roman soldiers had the right to force civilians to carry their equipment for one mile. But the law was quite strict; it forbade them to make someone go more than that. Turn the tables on them, advises Jesus. Don't fret and fume and plot revenge. Copy your generous God! Go a second mile, and astonish the soldier (and perhaps alarm him – what if his commanding officer found out?) with the news that there is a different way to be human, a way which doesn't plot revenge, which doesn't join the armed resistance movement (that's what verse 39 means), but which wins God's kind of victory over violence and injustice.

These examples are only little sketches, like cartoons to give you the idea. Whatever situation you're in, you need to think it through for yourself. What would it mean to reflect God's generous love despite the pressure and provocation, despite your own anger and frustration?

Impossible? Well, yes, at one level. But again Jesus' teaching isn't just good advice, it's **good *news*.** Jesus did it all himself, and opened up the new way of being human so that all who follow him can discover it. When they mocked him, he didn't respond. When they challenged him, he told quizzical, sometimes humorous, stories that forced them to think differently. When they struck him, he took the pain. When they put the worst bit of Roman equipment on his back – the heavy crosspiece on which he would be killed – he carried it out of the city to the place of his own execution. When they nailed him to the cross, he prayed for them.

The Sermon on the Mount isn't just about us. If it was, we might admire it as a fine bit of idealism, but we'd then return to our normal lives. It's about Jesus himself. This was the blueprint for his own life. He asks nothing of his followers that he hasn't faced himself. And, within his own life, we can already sense a theme that will grow larger and larger until we can't miss it. If this is the way to show what God is really like, and if this is the pattern that Jesus himself followed exactly, Matthew is inviting us to draw the conclusion: that in Jesus we see the Emmanuel, the God-with-us person. The Sermon on the Mount isn't just about how to behave. It's about discovering the living God in the loving, and dying, Jesus, and learning to reflect that love ourselves into the world that needs it so badly.

MATTHEW 6.1–6

Piety in Secret

[1]'When you are practising your piety, mind you don't do it with an eye on the audience! Otherwise, you won't have any reward from your father in heaven.

[2]'So when you give money to the poor, don't sound a trumpet in front of you. That's what people do when they're just play-acting, in the synagogues and the streets. They do it so that people will be impressed at them. I'm telling you the truth: they've received their reward in full. [3]No: when you give money, don't let your left hand have any idea what your right

hand is up to. ⁴That way, your giving will be in secret. And your father, who sees in secret, will repay you.

⁵'When you pray, you mustn't be like the play-actors. They love to pray standing in the synagogues and on street corners, so that people will notice them. I'm telling you the truth: they have received their reward in full. ⁶No: when you pray, go into your own room, shut the door, and pray to your father who is there in secret. And your father, who sees in secret, will repay you.'

Once, when living in the Middle East, I went out for a walk in the afternoon. On my way home, feeling slightly hungry, I bought a bar of chocolate at a wayside stall. I got back home, went to my room, made a cup of tea, unwrapped the chocolate and broke off a piece to eat it. Fortunately I glanced down at the chocolate before I put it in my mouth. When I did so I dropped it with a shout. It was alive. Inside what looked like a perfectly ordinary bar of chocolate were hundreds of tiny wriggling worms.

Jesus didn't know about chocolate, but he did know about things that looked fine on the outside but were rotten on the inside. Here, at the heart of the Sermon on the Mount, we find his shrewd comments on what it means to live a life that is, so to speak, solid chocolate all the way through.

The word 'piety' in the first verse is actually the same as the word '**covenant** behaviour' in 5.20. It's a many-sided word, especially in Matthew's **gospel**, but at the centre of it is the sense of the obligation which Israel had to God because of being his special people. In chapter 5, this focuses more on the **law**, and on what it means to keep (or not to break) that law in one's inner life and motivation. Now, in chapter 6, the focus is, to begin with, on the three things that Jews saw, and still see, as standard obligations: giving money, praying and fasting. In each case (we shall come to fasting presently) Jesus' point is the same. What matters is the motive. If these religious duties are done with an eye on the audience, they become rotten at the core.

Jesus doesn't say that these outward things don't matter. Giving money to those in need, praying to God day by day, and fasting when it's appropriate – he assumes that people will continue to do all of these. What matters is learning to do them simply to and for God himself. All the Sermon on the Mount, in fact, is centred on God himself, who easily gets squeezed out of religion if we're not careful.

Jesus also assumes that there is benefit to be had from doing these things. Many people imagine that he is asking us to do everything with no thought of reward, and are then rather shocked when he repeats, three times, his belief that our heavenly father will repay us (verses 4, 6, 18). Clearly, Jesus is not so bothered about the notion of disinterested behaviour, or 'altruism', as we sometimes are. In fact, what he says is far more realistic. If we struggle to clear our hearts of any desire to do something, so that we are acting from totally pure motives, we will always find a little corner of desire somewhere – even the desire to behave altruistically! Then, instead of looking away from ourselves and towards God, we find ourselves focusing back on ourselves again, wanting to please not God but our own ideal of lofty, disinterested action.

Jesus, instead, wants us to be so eager to love and please God that we will do everything we should do for his eyes alone. Other eyes will be watching from time to time, and it's very easy, particularly for clergy and others who are involved professionally with leading worship, to 'perform' for them rather than for God alone.

For that reason he gives quite specific instructions about how to be sure of integrity, of the outward appearance being matched by the inner reality. When you give money away, do your best simply to forget about it. You may have to record it in your tax return, but even that could suggest a calculating spirit, and the point here is to match the outgoing, spontaneous generosity of God himself. The best way to be sure is for nobody else to know.

The same applies to prayer. What you are in private is what you really are. Go into your inner room and talk to your father. You don't have to make a song and dance about it, and indeed the fewer people that know you're doing it the better. Nor do you have to go on mouthing pious phrases. You may find there are forms of words which help, as a framework or a starting-point; Jesus is about to give the **disciples** the framework he particularly recommends. But the point is to do business with God, one to one.

Jesus doesn't say what kind of reward we should expect. That, too, is part of the point. Simply knowing God better is reward enough; but there may be other things as well. You never know till you try. What is clear is that he is inviting his followers to a life in which inside and outside match perfectly, because both are focused on the God who sees in secret.

MATTHEW 6.7–15

The Lord's Prayer

[7]'When you pray, don't pile up a jumbled heap of words! That's what the Gentiles do. They reckon that the more they say, the more likely they are to be heard. [8]So don't be like them. You see, your father knows what you need before you ask him.
[9]'So this is how you should pray:

Our father in heaven,
May your name be honoured
[10]*May your kingdom come*
May your will be done
As in heaven, so on earth.
[11]*Give us today the bread we need now;*
[12]*And forgive us the things we owe,*

As we too have forgiven what was owed to us.
¹³*Don't bring us into the great Trial,*
But rescue us from evil.

¹⁴'Yes: if you forgive people the wrong they have done, your heavenly father will forgive you as well. ¹⁵But if you don't forgive people, neither will your heavenly father forgive you what you have done wrong.'

I was talking to a friend who had the reputation of being one of the finest preachers in the area. How did he go about it, I asked. He had no particular technique, he said; he just puzzled over the biblical readings that were set for that day until a framework emerged. Once he'd got a framework it was just a matter of writing it out.

That, of course, was a deceptively simple answer, and we can only guess at the hours of struggle and prayer that were disguised by such a short, and humble, response. But it's often the case, in many areas of life, that we blunder around until we find a framework around which we can build. And this is almost always true with prayer.

Jesus contrasts the sort of praying he has in mind with the sort that went on in much of the non-Jewish world. We know from many writings and inscriptions that many non-Jews did indeed use multiple formulae in their prayers: long, complicated magic words which they would repeat over and over in their anxiety to persuade some god or goddess to be favourable to them. Such prayers are often marked by a note of uncertainty. There were many divinities in the ancient pagan world, and nobody quite knew which one might need pacifying next, or with what formula.

This is hardly surprising. Prayer is one of life's great mysteries. Most people pray at least sometimes; some people, in many very different religious traditions, pray a great deal. At its lowest, prayer is shouting into a void on the off-chance there may be someone out there listening. At its highest, prayer merges into love, as the presence of God becomes so real that we pass beyond words and into a sense of his reality, generosity, delight and grace. For most Christians, most of the time, it takes place somewhere in between those two extremes. To be frank, for many people it is not just a mystery but a puzzle. They know they ought to do it but they aren't quite sure how.

What the Lord's Prayer provides, here at the heart of the Sermon on the Mount, is a *framework*. Jesus doesn't say you should always use identical words, and actually when Luke gives his version of the prayer it is different in small but interesting ways (Luke 11.2–4). It looks as though Jesus intended this sequence of thought to act more like the scaffolding than the whole building, though of course the prayer is used as it stands (usually in the longer version we find here in Matthew) by countless Christians every day. Already by Jesus' day the Jewish patterns of prayer were well established, with short but powerful prayers to be said three times a day. Maybe Jesus intended this prayer to be used like that as well.

What then does the prayer tell us about our regular approach to God? First, and so obvious that we might miss it, the prayer is deeply *meaningful*. It isn't a magic formula, an 'abracadabra', which plugs into some secret charm or spell. It is something we can mean with our minds (though it will stretch our thinking) as well as say with our lips. It implies strongly that we humans can and should use our ordinary language in talking to the creator of the universe, and that he wants and intends us to do so. It implies, in other words, that we share with the one true God a world of meaning which he wants us to explore.

Second, everything is set within our calling God 'father' (as Jesus does throughout this Sermon – in fact, we could suggest that a title for the whole Sermon might be, 'What it means to call God "father"'). For Jews in Jesus' day, this title for God went back to God's action in the **Exodus**, rescuing Israel from Egypt and so demonstrating that 'Israel is my son, my first-born' (Exodus 4.22).

Third, this God is not a man-made idol. He is the living God, who dwells in '**heaven**', and longs to see his sovereign and saving rule come to birth on 'earth'. This is, in fact, a prayer for the **kingdom of God** to become fully present: not for God's people to be snatched away from earth to heaven, but for the glory and beauty of heaven to be turned into earthly reality as well. When that is done, God's name – his character, his reputation, his very presence – will be held in high honour everywhere. The first half of the prayer is thus all about God. Prayer that doesn't start there is always in danger of concentrating on ourselves, and very soon it stops being prayer altogether and collapses into the random thoughts, fears and longings of our own minds.

Fourth, though, because this God is the creator, who loves his world and his human creatures, we can ask him for everything we need in the safe knowledge that he is far more concerned about it all even than we are ourselves. Much of the rest of the chapter spells this out. But if we are truly praying this prayer to God's honour, we can never simply pray for food for ourselves. We must pray for the needs of the whole world, where millions go hungry and many starve. And already we may sense, bubbling up out of the prayer, the realization that if we truly pray it we might also have to do something about it, to become part of God's answer to our own praying. But more of that in due course.

Fifth, we pray for forgiveness. Unlike some religions, in which every single action carries eternal and unbreakable consequences, at the heart of Judaism and Christianity lies the belief that, though human actions matter very deeply, forgiveness is possible and, through God's love, can become actual. Jesus assumes that we will need to ask for forgiveness not on one or two rare occasions but very regularly. This is a sobering thought, but it is matched by the comforting news that forgiveness is freely available as often as we need it.

There is, however, a condition, which remarkably enough is brought right into the prayer itself: we ourselves must be forgiving people. Jesus takes an extra moment afterwards to explain why. The heart that will not open to forgive others will remain closed when God's own forgiveness is offered. Jesus will say more about this in chapter 18.

The prayer ends with a sombre and realistic note. Jesus believed that the great time of testing was coming upon the world, and that he would have to walk alone into its darkness. His followers should pray to be spared it. Even now, in the light of Easter and with the guidance and power of the **Holy Spirit**, we still need to pray in this way. There will come yet more times of crisis, times when all seems dark for the world, the church, and in our own hearts and lives. If we follow a crucified **Messiah**, we shouldn't expect to be spared the darkness ourselves. But we must, and may, pray to be kept from its worst ravages, and to be delivered from evil, both in the abstract and in its personified form, 'the evil one'.

Here is the framework Jesus knew we would need. Here is your heavenly father waiting and longing for you to use it day by day as you grow in your knowledge, love and service of him. What is stopping you from making it your own?

MATTHEW 6.16–24

On Fasting and Lasting Treasure

[16]'When you fast, don't be gloomy like the play-actors. They make their faces quite unrecognizable, so that everyone can see they're fasting. I'm telling you the truth: they have received their reward in full. [17]No: when you fast, tidy your hair and

beard the way you normally do, and wash your face, [18]so that others won't notice you're fasting – except your father, privately. Then your father, who sees in private, will repay you.

[19]'Don't store up treasure on earth. Moths and rust will eat it away, and robbers will break in and steal it. [20]No: store up for yourselves treasure in heaven! Moths and rust don't eat it away there, and no robbers break in and steal it. [21]Show me your treasure, and I'll show you where your heart is.

[22]'The eye is the lamp of the body. So if your eye is honest and clear, your whole body will be full of light. [23]But if your eye is evil, your whole body is in the dark. So, if the light within you turns out to be darkness, darkness doesn't come any darker than that.

[24]'Nobody can serve two masters. Otherwise, they will either hate the first and love the second, or be devoted to the first and despise the second. You can't serve both God and wealth.'

The student looked crestfallen, as well he might. For weeks he had thought he was doing all right. Yes, he hadn't been working as hard as he could have done; but he was in the college football team, and he was playing in a rock group, and he was reading some very exciting novels . . . and somehow he hadn't been spending quite as much time in the library as most of the others. Now his tutor was facing him with the question. What were his priorities? Did he want to get a university education and degree, or did he just want to be at a wonderful holiday camp?

Of course, many students manage to juggle dozens of different commitments and still end up doing enough work to earn a degree. But frequently they have to face difficult choices. A bright, energetic young person could in theory do any one of several dozen things in any given week, but there are only so many hours in the day and you can't do everything. What is really important? What will you say, when you look back in ten years' time? 'I wish I'd really given it my best shot'? or 'I'm glad I decided to put all my effort into it'?

This passage is about priorities, and the central priority is God himself. No question about the importance of putting God first. But the catch is that, because God is loving and gentle, and wants us to choose to love and serve him freely rather than to be forced into it like slaves, it often seems, even to Christians who have in principle decided to give their lives to him, that there are many different things they could do. And often the different things start to take over . . . not least when they make money or bring fame. This passage is all about learning to love and serve God for himself, and in secret, rather than simply having an eye on the main chance, either to show off by being so religious or to store up wealth.

The opening paragraph picks up the same theme that we found in the earlier passages about money and prayer. Jesus assumes that his followers are going to fast from time to time, as part of their prayer and devotion to God. Later on (9.14–15) he explains that this won't be the right thing to do while he is there with them, but hints that it will be once he's gone. But the question is, how?

The current practice of Jesus' day seems to have been to advertise one's fasting by letting your hair (and beard) go tangled, and by smearing ashes on your face. That's just play-acting, Jesus declares. It's putting on a mask. Real fasting is between you and God, not something you do to show off. So do what you normally do to your head and face – wash, comb, sort yourself out in the usual way (in his culture that included anointing with oil, and that's what this passage literally means). The important point, here and all through, is the question: is your eye fixed on God, or on someone (or something) else? What is your priority?

The three little sayings which follow all make the same point. First, Jesus points out the difference between two sorts of treasure. As with other references to **heaven** and earth, we shouldn't imagine he means 'don't worry about this life – get ready for the next one'. 'Heaven' here is where God is right now, and where, if you learn to love and serve God right now, you will have treasure in the present, not just in the future. Of course Jesus (like almost all Jews of his day) believed that after death God would have a wonderful future in store for his faithful people; but they didn't normally refer to that future as 'heaven'. He wanted his followers to establish heavenly treasure right now, treasure which they could enjoy in the present as well as the future, treasure that wasn't subject to the problems that face all earthly hoards. How can one do this? Well, the whole chapter so far gives us the clue. Learn to live in the presence of the loving father. Learn to do everything for him and him alone. Get your priorities right.

Second, make sure your lamp is shedding light, not darkness. This is a tricky little saying. What does Jesus mean by saying that the eye is the lamp of the body?

Three things, I think. First, he means that we must, as we say, 'keep our eyes fixed on God'. Since we can't actually see God, that is picture-language, but we know what he means.

Second, though, I think Jesus literally meant that we should take care what we actually look at. Where do your eyes naturally get drawn to? Are you in control of them, or do they take you – and your mind and heart – wherever they want?

Third, the eyes are like the headlights of a car. Supposing you're driving along a dark road at night, and you try to switch the lights on – and nothing happens! You suddenly realize just how dark it really is. That's what it's like, Jesus is saying, if your eyes are not on God, and if instead they are following whatever eye-catching, pretty thing happens to take their fancy. Priorities again. Are your eyes leading you in the right direction, and showing you the road ahead?

Finally, the best known of these sayings. You can't serve

God and . . . mammon, say the older translations. 'Mammon' was a way of referring to property and wealth in general, almost as though it were a god – which is precisely Jesus' point here. We make the same point by saying things like 'The Almighty Dollar' (dangerously like 'Almighty God'). We joke about money because we are all too aware of its power: 'Money talks,' says the comedian, 'but what it mostly says to me is, "Good-bye!"' But what Jesus is saying is that money gives orders. It bosses you around. If you have your priorities right, there is only one boss, and that is God himself.

Sort your priorities out. When you look back at your life in two, five, ten, fifteen years' time, will you be glad you put first things first?

MATTHEW 6.25–34

Do Not Worry

[25]So let me tell you: don't worry about your life – what to eat, what to drink; don't worry about your body – what to wear. There's more to life than food! There's more to the body than a suit of clothes! [26]Have a good look at the birds in the sky. They don't plant seeds, they don't bring in the harvest, they don't store things in barns – and your father in heaven feeds them! Think how different you are to them! [27]Can any of you add fifteen inches to your height just by worrying about it?

[28]And why worry about what to wear? Take a tip from the lilies in the countryside. They don't work; they don't weave; [29]but, let me tell you, not even Solomon in all his finery was dressed as well as one of these. [30]So if God gives that sort of clothing even to the grass in the field, which is here today and on the bonfire tomorrow, isn't he going to clothe you too, you little-faith lot?

[31]'So don't worry away with your "What'll we eat?" and "What'll we drink?" and "What'll we wear?" [32]Those are the all the kinds of things the Gentiles fuss about, and your heavenly

father knows you need them all. [33]Instead, make your top priority God's kingdom and his way of life, and all these things will be given to you as well.

[34]'So don't worry about tomorrow. Tomorrow can worry about itself. One day's trouble at a time is quite enough.'

Has it ever struck you what a basically *happy* person Jesus was?

Oh yes, we know that, according to the prophecies, he was 'a man of sorrow, and acquainted with grief'. We know that the darkness and sadness of all the world descended on him as he went to the cross. The scene in Gethsemane, where he is wrestling with his father's will, and in agony wondering if he's come the right way, is one of the most harrowing stories ever told. We know that he wept at the tomb of Lazarus, and that he was sad when people refused to trust God and see the wonderful things he was doing.

But these are the exceptions, the dark patches painted on to the bright background. As we read a passage like this, we should see that it flows straight out of Jesus' own experience of life. He had watched the birds wheeling around, high up on the currents of air in the Galilean hills, simply enjoying being alive. He had figured out that they never seemed to do the sort of work that humans did, and yet they mostly stayed alive and well. He had watched a thousand different kinds of flowers growing in the fertile Galilee soil – the word translated 'lily' here includes several different plants, such as the autumn crocus, the anemone and the gladiolus – and had held his breath at their fragile beauty. One sweep of a scythe, one passing donkey, and this wonderful object, worth putting in an art gallery, is gone. Where did its beauty come from? It didn't spend hours in front of the mirror putting on make-up. It didn't go shopping in the market for fine clothes. It was just itself: glorious, God-given, beautiful.

Jesus had a strong, lively sense of the goodness of his father, the creator of the world. His whole spirituality is many a mile from those teachers who insisted that the present world was a place of shadows, gloom and vanity, and that true philosophy consisted in escaping it and concentrating on the things of the mind. His teaching grew out of his own experience. When he told his followers not to worry about tomorrow, we must assume he led them by example. He wasn't always looking ahead anxiously, making the present moment count only because of what might come next. No: he seems to have had the skill of living totally in the present, giving attention totally to the present task, celebrating the goodness of God here and now. If that's not a recipe for happiness, I don't know what is.

And he wanted his followers to be the same. When he urged them to make God their priority, it's important to realize which God he's talking about. He's not talking about a god who is distant from the world, who doesn't care about beauty and life and food and clothes. He's talking about the creator himself, who has filled the world with wonderful and mysterious things, full of beauty and energy and excitement, and who wants his human creatures above all to trust him and love him and receive their own beauty, energy and excitement from him.

So when Jesus tells us not to worry about what to eat, or drink, or wear, he doesn't mean that these things don't matter. He doesn't mean that we should prefer (as some teachers have suggested) to eat and drink as little as possible, and to wear the most ragged and disreputable clothes, just to show that we despise such things. Far from it! Jesus liked a party as much as anyone, and when he died the soldiers so admired his tunic that they threw dice for it rather than tearing it up. But the point was again priorities. Put the world first, and you'll find it gets moth-eaten in your hands. Put God first, and you'll get the world thrown in.

Nor does Jesus mean, of course, that we should not plant

seeds and reap harvests, or that we should not work at weaving and spinning to make clothes. Rather, we should do these things with joy, because our God, our father, is the creator of all and wants to feed and clothe us – not gloomily, as though God were a mean tyrant who was out to get us and make life difficult for us. Of course, because we live in a world filled with anxiety, it's easy to let it rub off on us. But the underlying principles of the whole Sermon on the Mount come together at this point in a huge but exhilarating challenge. God's **kingdom**, and the way of life that goes with it; the 'righteousness', or **covenant** behaviour, the way of life, that marks out God's people; these are the things you should aim at. Then you'll find that food, drink and clothing look after themselves.

Living totally without worry sounds, to many people, as impossible as living totally without breathing. Some people are so hooked on worry that if they haven't got anything to worry about they worry that they've forgotten something. Here, at the heart of the Sermon on the Mount, is an invitation that surprisingly few people even try to take up. Why not learn how to share the happiness of Jesus himself?

MATTHEW 7.1–6

On Judging Others

[1]'Don't judge people, and you won't be judged yourself. [2]You'll be judged, you see, by the judgment you use to judge others! You'll be measured by the measuring-rod you use to measure others! [3]Why do you stare at the speck of dust in your neighbour's eye, but ignore the plank in your own? [4]How can you say to your neighbour, "Here – let me get that speck of dust out of your eye," when you've got the plank in your own? [5]You're just play-acting! First take the plank out of your own eye, and then you'll see clearly enough to take the speck out of your neighbour's eye.

> ⁶'Don't give holy things to dogs. Don't throw your pearls to pigs. If you do, they will trample them under their feet – and then turn round and attack you!'

William Shakespeare based a whole play on the second verse of Matthew 7. *Measure for Measure* is classified as a 'comedy', and indeed everything works out very well in the end. But much of the play is dark and disturbing.

Angelo, a noble but stern lord, is left in charge of Vienna while Vincentio, the Duke, goes away for a spell. At least, he pretends to go away, but actually he stays near at hand, in disguise. No sooner has Angelo taken power than, obeying the Duke's instructions, he tightens up the ancient laws, condemning to death one Claudio, who has fathered a child out of wedlock. Isabella, the condemned man's sister, pleads for his life, warning Angelo that judgment from God himself is impartial, and that he too may find himself in need of the mercy which God provided in Christ:

> Why, all the souls that were were forfeit once;
> And He that might the vantage best have took
> Found out the remedy. How would you be
> If He, which is the top of judgment, should
> But judge you as you are? O, think on that;
> And mercy then will breathe within your lips,
> Like man new made.
>
> *Measure for Measure* Act 2, Scene 2

Angelo refuses: Claudio must die. But at the same time Angelo is smitten by a passionate lust for Isabella herself, and offers to spare her brother if only she will allow him to have his way with her. The plot twists and turns, but ends with Angelo, his own vice having been exposed, pleading for the death he richly deserves. But the Duke, weaving the threads of the story together, pardons one and all, while at the same time a deep and rich justice is done.

Shakespeare hints throughout at the Christian meanings of justice and mercy. The sovereign God, who seems to be absent from the world, is in fact present, supremely of course in Jesus himself. He takes human sin and self-righteousness, exposes them and deals with them, and yet allows mercy to triumph gloriously over justice. There is a mystery here which deserves much pondering.

This is the mystery that lies underneath the present passage. Jesus warns sternly against condemning others. Of course, this does not mean (as some have thought) that no follower of Jesus should ever be a magistrate. God intends that his world should be ordered, and that injustice should be held in check. Jesus is referring, not to official lawcourts, but to the judgments and condemnations that occur within ordinary lives, as people set themselves up as moral guardians and critics of one another.

We rightly guess that he had a particular target in mind. In 5.20 he has named them: the **scribes** and **Pharisees**. Though we know from history, and from the New Testament itself, that there were many scribes and Pharisees who were genuinely and humbly pious people, the tendency of hard-line pressure-groups – which is what the Pharisees basically were – is always to create a moral climate in which everybody looks at everybody else to see if they are keeping their standards up.

In many countries, this kind of moral climate used to be maintained in relation to sexual morality. Often, today, the moralism is just as fierce, but the target has changed. Today it might be, for instance, conservation and the environment. In some countries, neighbours spy on each other to make sure they place the right kind of garbage in the right kind of bag, so concerned are they about proper disposal and the danger of pollution. That word, in fact, is an indication of what's going on: 'pollution' was precisely what the Pharisees were afraid of.

Jesus warns against all such 'judgment'. He doesn't mean that we shouldn't have high standards of behaviour for ourselves and our world, but that the temptation to look down on each other for moral failures is itself a temptation to play God. And, since we aren't God, that means it's a temptation to play a part, to act, to be a 'hypocrite' (which literally means a play-actor, one who wears a mask as a disguise).

With the warning example of Angelo before us, we can see what will happen to such people. Judgment will bounce back on them, the measuring-stick they use for others will be lined up against them, and, while they patronizingly try to sort out other people's problems, their own will loom so large that they won't be able to see straight. Jesus, we should note, doesn't rule out the possibility that some people will eventually be able to help others to take specks of dust out of their eyes. He isn't saying that there is no such thing as public morality. But he is warning that the very people who seem most eager to tell others what to do (or more likely what not to do) are the people who should take a long look in the mirror before they begin.

What then about the dogs, the pigs and the pearls? Doesn't this imply that Jesus' followers are to make quite a serious judgment – namely that some people come into these categories, so should not be given holy or precious things?

Yes. It seems as though Jesus is here assuming a distinction between one's own community – in his case that of village and town life in Galilee, within the Jewish world of his day – and people from outside. 'Dogs' was after all a regular abusive term for **Gentiles**; pigs were kept only by Gentiles, since Jews didn't eat pork. He seems to be warning his followers not to try to explain the meaning and life of the **kingdom** to people who won't even understand the Jewish world within which it makes sense.

If this is right, it fits with what Jesus says later, in 10.5–6. The early mission of the **gospel** is to Jews only (see too Romans 15.8). After the crucifixion and **resurrection**, of course, everything is different; the gospel must then go out to embrace the world. For the moment, the **disciples** are to treasure the gospel like **priests** in the **Temple** guarding their holy things. Even though we live today in the new world, commanded to share the gospel riches with all and sundry, it would be good to think we still regarded the message of the kingdom as something sacred and beautiful, to be treasured and valued.

MATTHEW 7.7–12

On Prayer

[7]'Ask and it will be given to you! Search and you will find! Knock and the door will be opened for you! [8]Everyone who asks receives; everyone who searches finds; everyone who knocks will have the door opened. [9]Don't you see? Supposing your son asks you for bread – which of you is going to give him a stone? [10]Or if he asks for a fish, are you going to give him a serpent? [11]Well then: if you know how to give good gifts to your children, evil as you are, how much more will your father in heaven give good things to those who ask him!

[12]'So whatever you want people to do to you, do just that to them. Yes; this is what the law and the prophets are all about.'

I hate fundraising. Many people are good at it; many actually enjoy it; but I can't stand it. I hate asking people for things anyway, and asking for money is the worst of all. As a result, I'm not very good at it. I understand that in some countries it's expected that clergy, and people in similar jobs, should cheerfully ask people to give to good causes. In my world, it always seems difficult and embarrassing.

So when I read a passage like this I find it very hard to believe, and I have to remind myself of what it's based on.

Does Jesus *really* mean that God is going to answer every request we make? That he is like a father longing to give his children what they want and need? Can we truly take him up on such remarkably open-ended promises?

I think sometimes our failure to believe such promises, and to act on them, doesn't come so much from a failure of **faith** in God but from a natural human reluctance, like my dislike of fundraising. Maybe I was taught when I was little not to go on asking for things all the time. It's too long ago to remember. But I suspect many people have that instinctive reluctance to ask for things; if pressed, they might say it was selfish, or that God had better things to do with his time than to provide whatever we suddenly happen to want.

Well, that may or may not be true, but it would be a shame to tone down one of the most sparkling and generous sets of promises anywhere in the Bible. Maybe it isn't 'selfish' to ask for things. Maybe it's just the natural thing that children are supposed to do with parents. Maybe our refusal to do so actually makes God sad or puzzled: why aren't his children telling him how it is for them, what they'd like him to do for them? Of course, generosity of spirit is easily abused, and we all know the caricatures of people asking God for wildly inappropriate things in order simply to indulge themselves ('O Lord,' pleads the song, 'Won't you buy me – a Mercedes-Benz?')! The letter of James (4.3) has some stern warnings about asking for the wrong sort of things, and any full discussion of prayer needs to take this into account. But, for most of us, the problem is not that we are too eager to ask for the wrong things. The problem is that we are not nearly eager enough to ask for the right things.

And 'the right things' doesn't simply mean fine moral qualities (though if you dare to pray for holiness, humility or other dangerous things, God may just give them to you). It means the things we need day by day, which God is just as concerned about as we are. If he is a father, let's treat him as a father, not a bureaucrat or dictator who wouldn't want to be bothered with our trivial and irrelevant concerns. It's up to him to decide if he's too busy for us. The fact that there may be a war going on in one country, a famine somewhere else, earthquakes, tragic accidents, murder and pillage all over the place, and that he is grieving over all of them – this might be a problem for a high-ranking authority at the United Nations, but it is no problem whatever for our loving father. When he says he's still got time, space and love to spare for us, we should take him at his word.

Of course, as we become mature children we will increasingly share his concerns for his suffering and sorrowing world. We will want to pray for it more than for ourselves. But, within the **kingdom**-prayer that Jesus taught us, as well as praying for God's will to be done on earth, we were taught to pray for what we ourselves need here and now. So: what's stopping us?

We may well say that we've tried it and it didn't work. Well, prayer remains a mystery. Sometimes when God seems to answer 'no' we find it puzzling. And people have always found it strange that, if God is supremely wise, powerful and loving, he shouldn't simply do for everybody everything that they could possibly want. But, as Archbishop William Temple famously said, 'When I pray, coincidences happen; when I stop praying, the coincidences stop happening.' Some of the wisest thinkers of today's church have cautiously concluded that, as God's kingdom comes, it isn't God's will to bring it all at once. We couldn't bear it if he did. God is working like an artist with difficult material; *and prayer is the way some of that material co-operates with the artist instead of resisting him.* How that is so we shall never fully understand until we see God face to face. That it is so is one of the most basic Chrisian insights.

So: treat God as a father, and let him know how things are

with you! Ask, search and knock and see what happens! Expect some surprises on the way, but don't expect that God will ever let you down. This, indeed, is the underlying message of the whole Sermon on the Mount, which is now moving towards its closing paragraphs.

Verse 12, in fact, sums up the message so far, the message which began at 5.17–20. Jesus hasn't come to abolish, but to fulfil, the **law** and the prophets. How? By teaching Israel who God really is, and what copying him, trusting him, loving and obeying him are really like. And, when it comes to behaviour in the world, and with other people, the whole law can be put into one sentence: do to others what you'd like them to do to you.

Jesus was neither the first nor the last great moral teacher to offer this so-called 'Golden Rule', and it sums up a good deal of his teaching. What distinguishes him from the many others who have said similar things is that underneath the moral lesson is the love of the heavenly father. What should distinguish his followers, but alas frequently doesn't, is that, knowing this love, they should find themselves able to obey this rule, and the other rules that follow from it, gladly and freely. They should then discover that they are able to reflect God's love and light into the world.

MATTHEW 7.13–23

The Two Ways

[13]'Go in by the narrow gate. The gate that leads to destruction, you see, is nice and wide, and the road going there has plenty of room. Lots of people go that way. [14]But the gate leading to life is narrow, and the road going there is a tight squeeze. Not many people find their way through.

[15]'Watch out for false prophets. They will come to you dressed like sheep, but inside they are hungry wolves. [16]You'll

be able to tell them by the fruit they bear: you don't find grapes growing on thorn-bushes, do you, or figs on thistles? [17]Well, in the same way, good trees produce good fruit, and bad trees produce bad fruit. [18]Actually, good trees *can't* produce bad fruit, nor can bad ones produce good fruit! [19]Every tree that doesn't produce good fruit is cut down and thrown on the fire. [20]So: you must recognize them by their fruits.

[21]'Not everyone who says to me, "Master, master" will enter the kingdom of heaven; only people who do the will of my father in heaven. [22]On that day lots of people will say to me,

'"Master, master – we prophesied in your name, didn't we? We cast out demons in your name! We performed lots of powerful deeds in your name!"

[23]'Then I will have to say to them,

'"I never knew you! You're a bunch of evildoers – go away from me!"'

Driving the car these days becomes more and more complicated. On any given stretch of road there are more and more warning signs. 'Lane closed.' 'Mud on Road.' 'Slow Farm Vehicles.' Not to mention signs telling you how fast you're allowed to drive, warning you there are police cameras waiting to catch you if you speed, suggesting you stop for a cup of coffee before you get too tired, and telling you how far it is to your destination.

Jesus ends the great Sermon on the Mount with a set of warning signs. If you've come this far with him, you need to know it's not just a matter of holding on to the steering wheel and hoping for the best. You need to concentrate, to take note of danger, to realize that you can't presume on anything. You've got to keep your wits about you.

This passage has three of these warnings, coming in quick succession like road-signs on a motorway. Make sure you get through the gate – it's not very wide! Watch out for people who will lead you off the road! Don't think that because

75

you've been tagging along with the others that you'll get there in the end! These are sharp and worrying. We need to take them seriously.

First, the narrow gate. The old walled city of Jerusalem still has several gates, some with wide roadways so that cars can get through, others with steep, narrow steps so that only pedestrians, animals and small handcarts can pass. Jesus' hearers would have been familiar with many towns and cities like that. Some city gates would be wide enough for several people to go in and out at once; at others you would have to wait your turn. Jesus sets his face against any idea that you can simply 'go with the flow', allowing the crowd to set the pace and the direction.

You really have to want to get in through this gate. If you just drift, allowing the current to take you where it will, you'll miss it. But this gate leads to life, and the other sort all lead to destruction. The choice is spelled out at last, and there's no avoiding it, no softening of the hard line. Choices matter; actions and motives matter. Learning to follow Jesus and to know God as father matter. Eternal issues are at stake. '**Heaven**', as I have stressed, is God's dimension, God's sphere of existence, in the present, not simply a destination in the future. But that doesn't mean that there aren't future destinies, or that yours is not going to be shaped by the choices you make in the present. And as soon as you hear a little voice saying 'maybe Jesus didn't mean it – surely he can't have been that strict – maybe it'll all come right in the end no matter what we do', you need the next warning.

The next warning, in line with biblical instructions, is against 'false prophets'. In ancient Israel, 'false prophets' were people who claimed to be speaking the word of **YHWH** but actually weren't. If people listened to them they would end up going the wrong way, and disaster would follow. But the trouble with false prophets is of course that they *seem* very nice, very reasonable, very trustworthy. No wolf is going to let you see his claws and teeth if he can dress himself up as a harmless sheep – and that's what they will do.

In the Old Testament, the test for true and false prophets was: wait and see! If the prophet tells you that something is going to happen, you will discover whether they are truthful by seeing whether it does. Jesus has a more graphic, and perhaps a quicker, method of detection. Look at the life of the person who is offering you advice. Think of it like a tree. Can you see healthy, tasty fruit on this tree? Can you see other people being genuinely nourished by it? Or is it, in fact, producing a crop of lies, immorality and greed?

Within the Christian church there is always a temptation to ask different questions about people. 'Is he one of us?' people enquire. 'Does she belong to my party, to our group, to the proper tradition?' But parties, groups and traditions have a way of attracting both genuine believers and true prophets on the one hand and false prophets and hangers-on on the other. The only way to be sure is to look for fruit from the tree, and to be sure what sort of fruit it is.

The 'fruit' cannot simply be showy displays of apparent spiritual power. False prophets can often produce that sort of thing. What counts is something deeper, something more personal. The final warning in this sequence moves our attention to the final day, the day of judgment. 'On that day' in verse 22 is the first use, but by no means the last in Matthew, of a regular phrase which Jesus has transferred from the Old Testament warnings about coming divine judgment into his own warnings about what would happen when God finally acted. Some, it seems, will have done remarkable things 'in Jesus' name' but without knowing him personally. Mighty deeds are not a final indication of whether someone really belongs to Jesus or not. There are some who will have done them, but who will turn out to be 'evil workers'. What counts will be knowing Jesus – or rather, being known by him. What does that mean? Read the rest of the story and find out.

MATTHEW 7.24–29

True Obedience

24'So, then, everyone who hears these words of mine and does them will be like a wise man who built his house on the rock. 25Heavy rain fell; floods rose up; the winds blew and beat on that house. It didn't fall, because it was founded on the rock. 26And everyone who hears these words of mine and doesn't do them – they will be like a foolish man, who built his house on sand. 27Heavy rain fell; floods rose up; the winds blew and battered the house – and it fell down! It fell with a great crash.'

28And so it was, when Jesus finished these words, that the crowds were astonished at his teaching. 29He was teaching them, you see, on his own authority, not like their scribes used to do.

There is a long-standing tradition among those who climb mountains in my part of the world. Often the hills, even the low ones, are covered in mist or cloud, and on many tracks and trails there is a good chance of getting lost and missing the way. So successive generations of hikers have built cairns: piles of stones, mostly quite small, marking the path, leading to a much larger pile at the summit itself – in case, in the mist, you aren't sure whether you've got there or not. Many times I have almost gone off in the wrong direction in thick fog, only to see a cairn at the last moment and come back on track.

Many readers of the New Testament, perhaps especially readers of the **gospels**, find themselves wandering through Jesus' teaching like someone climbing a hill in the mist. Lessons about this and that, Jesus meeting people, healing people, confronting people, giving more teaching. There seems to be so much of it, and we sometimes feel we need some way of marking the path we're really on as we read the gospel. Fortunately, that's exactly what Matthew has given us.

At this stage of the gospel, like somebody climbing in the hills for the first time, we probably don't realize what Matthew has done. But if we keep our wits about us we soon will. At the end of this passage, in verse 28, he rounds off the long Sermon on the Mount by commenting 'So, when Jesus had finished these words . . .'.

As it stands this is unremarkable. But then, three chapters later, we find a similar statement: 'So, when Jesus had finished teaching his twelve **disciples** . . .' (11.1). Maybe this is Matthew's idea of a cairn, telling us how to keep on the path? Yes! After the long chapter of parables, we find: 'So, when Jesus had finished these **parables** . . .' (13.53). Now we're getting the idea; one more and we're nearly there. 'So, when Jesus had finished these words . . .' (19.1); the same as the first one. Then, finally, with a sense of arrival: 'So, when Jesus had finished *all* these words . . .' (26.1). Step by step Matthew has led us up the mountain, until at last the clouds roll away and we find ourselves standing on the dizzy summit, understanding at last who Jesus is and what he's come to do.

This is how Matthew has marked off the five great blocks of teaching in his gospel. We are at the end of the Sermon on the Mount (chapters 5—7); chapter 10 consists of instructions to the disciples for their mission; chapter 13, of parables; chapter 18, of teachings about the community that is coming into being around Jesus and his ministry. Finally, chapters 23—25, a long section matching the Sermon on the Mount, picks up from the end of the opening Sermon the note of dire warning, and develops it in one picture after another of coming judgment.

Why has Matthew done this? What does this marking of the path tell us about what he thinks of Jesus?

The answer is found, as so often, in Matthew's echoes of the

Old Testament. Matthew has already coloured in his picture of Jesus by drawing on the stories of the **Exodus** from Egypt. Now he has had Jesus sitting on a hill instructing his followers – not quite like the thunder and lightning of Mount Sinai, but close enough to make people draw the parallel between him and Moses, going up the mountain and coming down with the **Torah**. But these are small-scale hints and nudges. What now comes into our view is a bird's-eye view of the whole gospel, arranged as a story containing five blocks of teaching – and, as every Jew knew, the first five books of the Bible were known as the 'five books of Moses', the 'Pentateuch'. One of the main things Matthew wants to tell us is that Jesus is like Moses – only more so.

That, of course, is why he could teach the people on his own authority. In Jesus' day, and ever since then, Jewish teachers have taught by starting with parts of the Torah and discussing what great teachers have made of them. Teaching becomes a matter of laying out what other people have said, rather than any individual teacher offering a brand new line of interpretation. But in the Sermon on the Mount Jesus is quite blunt: this, he says, is what *I* say to you. Never mind what you've heard from elsewhere. Never mind that the text has been read differently for over a thousand years. This is the way we have to read it now.

Jesus insists, in the great warning which closes the Sermon, that his hearers will be judged, not even on their direct response to God himself, but on whether they hear these words and do them, or whether they let their ears enjoy the sound of the words but then leave them as a memory without doing anything about them. Doing what Jesus says, or not doing it: this makes the difference between a house that stays standing in a storm and a house that falls with a great crash.

This parable is well known, and often sung about in Sunday schools. Build your house on the rock, says Jesus; and the rock is his own words, or rather, doing those words instead of merely hearing them. But we often miss what his first hearers would probably have heard behind the dramatic picture-language. Not far away from where he sat on that hillside, just a hundred miles or so away in Jerusalem, Herod's men were continuing to rebuild the **Temple**. They spoke of it as God's House, and declared that it was built upon the rock, proof against wind and weather. In the last great sermon in Matthew's gospel, Jesus warns that the Temple itself will come crashing down, because Israel as a whole had failed to respond to his message. Halfway through the gospel, in another dramatic moment, he promises that Peter's confession of **faith** will form the rock on which something very different will be built – the community that believes in him, Jesus, as **Messiah.**

Once we see this larger picture we can see more clearly what Matthew wants us to pick up here. This is a message for all of us: if we build our lives on Jesus' teaching, we will be part of the 'house' that lasts for ever. But it began as a very specific promise and warning to his own people in his own day. Much of Jesus' teaching is like that. We often discover more of what it means for us by discovering more of what it meant, very specifically, for them.

What sort of 'houses' are we building today, then, in our own lives and in our churches? Are we 'doing' Jesus' words, or only reading them, hearing them, and thinking how fine they are?

MATTHEW 8.1–13

The Healing of the Leper and the Centurion's Servant

[1]When Jesus came down from the hillside, large crowds followed him. [2]Suddenly a leper approached, and knelt down in front of him.

'Master,' he said, 'if you want, you can make me clean!'

[3]Jesus stretched out his hand and touched him.

'I do want to,' he said. 'Be clean!'

At once his leprosy was cured.

[4]'Take care', Jesus said to him, 'that you don't say anything to anyone. Instead, go and show yourself to the priest, and make the offering which Moses commanded. That will be a proof to them.'

[5]Jesus went into Capernaum. A centurion came up and pleaded with him.

[6]'Master,' he said, 'my servant is lying at home, paralysed. He's in a very bad state.'

[7]'I'll come and make him better,' said Jesus.

[8]'Master,' replied the centurion, 'I don't deserve to have you come under my roof! Just say the word, and my servant will be healed. [9]I know what authority's all about, you know – I've got soldiers answering to me, and I can say to one of them, "Go!" and he goes, and to another one, "Come here!" and he comes, and I can say, "Do this," to my slave, and he does it!'

[10]Jesus was fair amazed when he heard this.

'I'm telling you the truth,' he said to the people who were following. 'I haven't found faith like this – not even in Israel! [11]Let me tell you this: lots of people will come from East and West and join Abraham, Isaac and Jacob in the great party to celebrate the kingdom of heaven. [12]But the children of the kingdom will be thrown into outer darkness, where people will weep and gnash their teeth.'

[13]Then he turned to the centurion.

'Go home,' he said. 'Let it be for you as you believed.'

And his servant was healed at that very moment.

'Who's in charge here?'

The policeman suddenly appeared in the doorway. Everyone stood still. It had been a wonderful party up to that point; a bit riotous, perhaps, but great fun. Now, we guessed, one of the neighbours had complained about the noise.

The student whose house we were in looked sheepish. 'Well,

nobody's in charge exactly,' he said, 'but it's my house.'

'Well,' said the policeman, 'I'm in charge now; and I'm telling you this noise must stop right away.' With that, he left. And so did we. The party was over.

Of course he had the authority, whether we liked it or not. He had the uniform, the police radio, the law to back him up. He knew it and we knew it. It didn't take any special insight to see it, or courage to respond. That was just the way it was.

But when Jesus came down from the mountain after the Sermon he had no uniform. No structure to back him up. No one else to appeal to. Matthew told us, at the end of the previous chapter, that the crowds were astonished because, when Jesus taught, he appeared, like the policeman in the doorway, to have authority. But was he just trying it on? Was he really 'in charge'? What might that mean?

Matthew's next section (chapters 8 and 9, before the next block of teaching in chapter 10) is mostly about what Jesus' authority looked like in practice, on the street. And it begins with these two little stories, about the **leper** and the centurion's servant. In both cases, Jesus has the power to heal, but the point goes beyond that.

With the leper, Jesus is restoring and renewing a member of Israel. With the centurion, **faith** in Jesus' authority is already spreading to people outside Israel, as a sign of the wonderful gathering-in of the nations that God intends to bring about. Together these two stories make a small but complete window on the whole **gospel**.

Leprosy (the word covered several types of virulent skin diseases) meant not only sickness and disfigurement, but also social banishment. Leprosy was highly contagious. Sufferers had to stay well away from everybody else. Nobody approached them; nobody would dream of touching them. We can feel, then, the shudder going through the onlookers as Jesus reaches out and touches this poor man.

But you can also feel the thrill of warmth and **life** that came over the leper himself. Nobody had touched him for a long time, perhaps many years. He was, to his surprise, caught up suddenly in God's renewal movement, God's restoration of his people.

Jesus had come, he said, not to destroy the **law** but to fulfil it (5.17). The leper needed not only physical healing but reintegration into society, back into family and village life. It wouldn't be much good going home and claiming to be cured unless he had the official authorization. So Jesus tells him to go through the regular process: show yourself to the **priest**, and make the required offering. He needed to be restored as a full member of Israel. Restoring God's people was part of what the gospel was all about.

But an even bigger shock comes with the calm recognition, by a **Gentile** army commander living locally in Capernaum, that when it came to diseases Jesus possessed the same sort of authority that he himself possessed over soldiers and slaves. Jesus exclaims at how remarkable this is. The man has faith of a sort that Jesus hasn't found among his own people. 'Faith' is defined here, it seems, not as a general religious attitude to life, but as something much more specific: recognizing that Jesus possesses authority. Faith like that brings its own reward. As he has believed, so it happens.

Though Jesus was quite clear that the time for Gentiles to come flooding in to God's **kingdom** was not yet (see 10.5–6), he knew that it would happen soon enough, and he saw this man's faith as an advance sign of it. The great celebration party of the kingdom would take place, and the patriarchs, the great ancestors of Israel – Abraham, Isaac and Jacob – would be joined, as the scriptures had predicted, by a great multitude from around the world. But Jesus saw at the same time that, despite his own best efforts, many of his kinsfolk would refuse to believe, and so would find themselves excluded. This tension runs right through the gospel, right through the New Testament, and right through the world to this day.

The challenge for today's Christian is to ask: what does it mean to recognize, and submit to, the authority of Jesus himself? What does it mean to call him 'Lord' and live by that? There is nothing in the New Testament to suggest that 'faith' is a general awareness of a supernatural dimension, or a general trust in the goodness of some distant divinity, so that some might arrive at this through Jesus and others by some quite different route. 'Faith', in Christian terms, means believing precisely that the living God has entrusted his authority to Jesus himself, who is now exercising it for the salvation of the world (see 28.18). If the policeman used his authority to break up a student party, Jesus is using his to set in motion a much greater celebration. And he invites us all to share in it.

MATTHEW 8.14–22

On Following Jesus

[14]Jesus went into Peter's house. There he saw Peter's mother-in-law laid low with a fever. [15]He touched her hand. The fever left her, and she got up and waited on him.

[16]When evening came, they brought to him many people who were possessed by demons. He cast out the spirits with a word of command, and healed everyone who was sick. [17]This happened so that the word spoken by Isaiah the prophet might come true:

He himself took our weaknesses
And bore our diseases.

[18]When Jesus saw the crowd all around him, he told them to go across to the other side of the lake. [19]A scribe came up and spoke to him.

'Teacher,' he said, 'I will follow you wherever you go!'

²⁰Foxes have their dens,' replied Jesus, 'and the birds in the sky have their nests. But the son of man has nowhere he can lay his head.'

²¹'Master,' said another of his disciples, 'let me first go and see to my father's funeral.'

²²Follow me!' replied Jesus. 'And leave the dead to bury their own dead.'

What do you *always* do first thing in the morning?

For some, it will be shaving. For others, it will be making a cup of tea. For some, it will be vigorous exercise. For others, it will be reading the newspaper. Put it the other way: if someone forcibly prevented you from going through your normal morning routine, what would you miss most?

Now imagine what it would take, other than physical violence, to make you suddenly do everything differently. With most of us, it would be very bad news: an accident, a sudden illness or death in the family. If I received, early in the morning, a telephone call to say that a close family member had just been involved in a major accident, I wouldn't do any of my normal morning things. I would pull on whatever clothes I could grab and go to be with them as fast as I could.

For a devout Jew, in Jesus' day and in our own, one of the most solemn and sacred parts of the morning routine would be to say the basic Jewish prayer: 'Hear, O Israel, the Lord our God is the only Lord; and you shall love the Lord your God with all your heart . . .' It is a beautiful and haunting prayer, which has become woven into the very lifeblood of Jewish people for thousands of years. Saying this prayer is regarded by official Jewish teaching as the most important thing to do each day.

But there is one thing which takes precedence even over saying this prayer. According to the **rabbis**' teaching, when a man's father dies he has such a strong obligation to give him a proper burial that this comes first, before everything else – even before saying the 'Hear, O Israel' prayer.

So when Jesus found one of his followers saying that he had to go and organize his father's funeral, you'd have expected him to say, 'Oh well, of course, you must go and do that – and then come and follow me later.' What Jesus actually said is one of the most shocking things in the whole **gospel** story. 'Let the dead bury the dead,' he said: 'you must follow me right now.'

Of course, we don't know if the man's father had actually died yet. He may just have been getting older, perhaps becoming sick. The man may have been using his future obligation as a way of postponing following Jesus for some time, possibly for several years. He was, we may suppose, keeping his options open. But when the saying was remembered it rang like a warning bell through the Jewish hearts and minds of Jesus' hearers. What Jesus was doing was so important, so urgent, so immediate that it was the one thing that mattered. Whatever else you were thinking of doing, this comes first.

Jesus' sovereign authority sweeps on through this story like a fresh wind coming through the window and turning all the papers upside down. He heals Peter's mother-in-law; he then heals everyone who is brought to the house. But in this sequence we start to see, as well, a more rounded view of this authority. Jesus doesn't have, as it were, absolute power for its own sake. He has authority *in order to be the healer*. And he is the healer by taking the sickness and pain of all the world on to himself. In verse 17 Matthew quotes from Isaiah 53.4, a passage more often associated in Christian thinking with the meaning of Jesus' death, bearing our griefs and sorrows on the cross; but for Matthew there is no sharp line between the healing Jesus offered during his life and the healing for sin and death which he offered through his own suffering. The one leads naturally into the other.

That is why Jesus issues a solemn warning to the enthusiastic **disciple** who proclaims that he will follow him wherever he goes. Do you really know, he says, what you're letting yourself in for? This isn't just an exciting and triumphant march, following the one who has God's authority, watching him do mighty and powerful things all over the place. This is a commitment to one whose authority is given in order that he can go to the places where the world is in its deepest pain, and be there with and for the people who are suffering it. Even foxes and birds have places to which they can go back when they're tired. Jesus will have none. He has a temporary home in Capernaum; but now he belongs on the road, in the countryside, in the streets and lanes, wherever God's people are in need. He will have no place to rest his head until at last it rests, lifeless, on the cross.

'The **son of man**', he said, 'has nowhere to lay his head.' By itself the phrase 'the son of man' here is very cryptic; it could simply mean 'I' or 'someone like me'. But for Matthew, who knows several other sayings in which this strange phrase occurs, there is no question: it carries the note of authority (see e.g. 9.6; 26.64). But it also speaks of suffering (20.28). Somehow, in Matthew's picture of Jesus, we find all this rolled together: authority *through* healing, healing *through* suffering. Authority and suffering are strangely concentrated in this one man, who nobody at this stage quite understood, but who everybody found compelling. Perhaps that's the greatest challenge facing the church today: how to live the life of Jesus, how to be his followers, in such a way that people will want to follow him too.

MATTHEW 8.23–27

The Calming of the Storm

[23]So Jesus got into the boat, and his disciples followed him. [24]All of a sudden a great storm blew up on the sea, so that the boat was being swamped by the waves. Jesus, however, was asleep. [25]They came and woke him up.

'Help, Master, help!' they shouted. 'We're done for!'

[26]'Why are you so scared, you little-faith lot?' he replied.

Then he got up and told the wind and the sea to behave themselves, and there was a great calm. [27]The people there were astonished.

'What sort of man is this,' they said, 'that the winds and the sea do what he says?'

The sea has always been a symbol of wild, untameable power. You only have to stand beside the ocean, even on a calm day, to sense something of it. There is so much of it, for a start; when the tide comes in, up a beach, imagine how many gallons of water have moved down the coastline; and it's doing that all the time, day and night. Then stand beside it when the wind gets up, and watch how all those millions of gallons leap and dance about like the water splashing in a child's bath. Then, if you dare, stand on the deck of a small boat as it sets out into those waves. Feel their power lift the boat high in the air and drop it down again with a crash and a smack. Watch the huge wave rise up, and up, in front of you, like a monster from a horror movie, alive and threatening.

The Jews were not, by and large, a seafaring people. Their neighbours to north and south, Phoenicia and Egypt, were maritime nations, trading widely across the Mediterranean world and beyond. But Israel concentrated on the land, which was after all their promised inheritance. The sea remained, in Jewish writing, a place and a power of darkness and evil, threatening and wild. Sometimes the sea appears as the primal element, the dark substance out of which, and in opposition to which, the creator God makes his beautiful world, winning a victory over the sea and all that it stands for. The stories about the sea in the Old Testament (there aren't many of them) make the same point: **YHWH** tames it at the **Exodus**, and uses it to stop the disobedient prophet Jonah in his tracks and send him back about his proper business. All of that is in the background as Matthew tells this story.

Indeed, the tale of the prophet Jonah is worth exploring a bit further to see just what's going on here. God told Jonah to go and preach in Nineveh. Jonah didn't want to, so he got on a boat going in the opposite direction. A great storm blew up, and the boat was in danger, but Jonah was asleep and didn't notice. They woke him up and told him to call on his god to do something. But Jonah knew what was going on. This was YHWH telling him he was out of line; he should have done what he had been told. So he instructed the sailors to throw him overboard. They did so, the storm subsided, and the sea became still. Meanwhile, Jonah was swallowed by a great fish, which then spat him out on dry land, after which he went off to Nineveh and carried out his commission.

This exciting and dramatic old story was certainly well known to Matthew and his readers, and one of the things he's doing is to say that Jesus is both like and unlike Jonah. This storm hasn't come up because he has refused to do what his father wanted. Rather, it becomes a further sign of his own authority. The **disciples** wake him up, but he doesn't have to call on anyone else, not even on his father, for help. Nor, of course, do they have to throw him overboard. In another, and greater, sign of his absolute authority, he simply rebukes the winds and the waves and they quieten down at once. If he is a prophet, he is a considerably greater one than Jonah, as Matthew will remind us later on (12.41). But, just as Jonah's extraordinary adventure was told as a sign that Israel's God did indeed care for everybody, not just Israel (Jonah's mission was to save Nineveh, a great pagan city, from imminent judgment), so these remarkable stories about Jesus are designed to show that what God was doing through him and in him was indeed nothing short of new creation.

That's why, once again, the proper reaction to Jesus is '**faith**'.

Again, this isn't a general religious response to the world around; a 'religious response' to a great storm at sea might be awe and terror, or frightened prayer to the sea-god. No: this 'faith' is quite simply a trust that Jesus is the sovereign one who has authority over the elements. And the disciples didn't have much of this faith. We now start to realize something which Matthew is telling us bit by bit: that other people (like the centurion at Capernaum) had a sharply focused and quite striking faith, and that Jesus' own followers, despite seeing all he had done, weren't yet in the same league.

They do, however, start to ask questions (verse 27). What does it mean? What sort of a man is this? They obviously regard him as a leader, as 'master'; they know he's a healer and teacher. But this goes way beyond anything they were expecting. Somehow his authority stretches not only to diseases – they'd heard of remarkable healers before, and were prepared to accept that kind of thing – but to the natural elements as well. Matthew keeps the question on the back burner, and proceeds to fill in the picture of Jesus' authority some more, before showing us gradually how the disciples came to a fuller understanding.

In the process, he wants us to ask two questions for ourselves. First, how do *we* regard Jesus? It's all very well to say in church, or in private devotion, that he's the **son of God**, the Lord, the **Messiah**, or whatever. Do we actually treat him as if he's got authority over every aspect of our lives and our world? Second, are we as his followers acting in such a way, in our confrontations with evil, our bold announcements of the **kingdom**, that other people say of us, What sort of people can they be?

MATTHEW 8.28–34

The Healing of the Demoniacs

²⁸So he went across to the other side, to the region of the Gadarenes. Two demon-possessed men met him, coming out

of the tombs. They were very violent and made it impossible for anyone to go along that road.

[29]'What is it with us and you,' they yelled, 'you son of God? Have you come here to torture us ahead of the time?'

[30]Some way off from where they were there was a large herd of pigs feeding.

[31]'If you cast us out,' the demons begged Jesus, 'send us into the herd of pigs!'

[32]'Off you go, then!' said Jesus.

So the demons went out of the men and into the pigs. Then and there the entire herd rushed down the steep slope into the lake, and were drowned in the water.

[33]The herdsmen took to their heels. They went off to the town and told the whole tale, including the bit about the demon-possessed men. [34]So the whole town came out to see Jesus for themselves. When they saw him, they begged him to leave their district.

I was listening to some music last night that kept surprising me. It was a great symphony, with a wonderful tune that turned this way and that, sweeping us along, catching our emotions and lifting our spirits. Then, just when you thought it couldn't go any further, something happened: a change of orchestration, a subtle shift in harmony, and we were on a different plane. Then, once more, it shifted, moving now a little faster, and a bit louder, with the music becoming more urgent and striking. Then a final change, so that you felt your whole body resonating and pulsing with the thrust and drive of it. Each stage had followed naturally from the previous one; yet, by the end, we had been taken from quite small beginnings to a massive climax of mood and emotion.

Matthew has been doing something similar throughout this chapter, and this story is the point where the music reaches its height. Glance back and you'll see. The chapter began with the little story of the **leper**: one man, a quick healing, important in its way but not particularly dramatic. Then the centurion and his servant: Jesus healing again, but this time at a distance, in response to remarkable **faith**, and with striking consequences (the prophecy of **Gentiles** flocking in to God's **kingdom**). Then some further stories of healing, deepening the mood and texture by pointing out the cost to Jesus himself, as he went his lonely way to the cross. Then the strong music swells and rises again with Jesus stilling the storm on the lake. And now, just when we thought it could get no stronger, we have the climax: the two demon-possessed men living among the tombs, shrieking madness and murder, ending with a herd of pigs rushing into the sea.

This story is, as it were, a yet more vivid version of the previous one (the stilling of the storm). Think of the wild sea, with wind and waves doing their worst. Now turn that into a human being, with the wind and waves inside them; not a bad image for how it is with some poor people who find that, for whatever reason, their imagination and emotions, their thinking and acting, seem to have been taken over by forces beyond their control.

Today we struggle, in the modern Western world, to explain what's going on inside people like that. In Jesus' world, and in many parts of our world today, the most natural explanation is that some evil force or forces has taken them over. '**Demons**', and possession by such creatures, was the regular way of describing that condition. Modern Western medicine has found alternative diagnoses for many people in this turbulent state; but there remain some for whom the ancient explanation still seems to be the best.

The point of this story, then, is that the Jesus who has authority to teach people, as he was doing in the Sermon on the Mount, also has authority over disease both close at hand and at a distance; over the lives of people who want to follow him; *and* over the winds and waves on the lake, and over the shadowy forces of evil, however we think about them or describe them. That's what we need to know as we ourselves sign on to follow him. He isn't just somebody with good ideas. He isn't just somebody who will tell us how to establish a better relationship with God. He is somebody with authority over everything that the physical world on the one hand, and the non-physical world on the other, can throw at us. This is a Jesus we can trust with every aspect of our lives.

We meet something in this story which we shall see again, later in Matthew. In the parallel stories in Mark and Luke, there is only one demon-possessed man; in Matthew, there are two. Various theories have been proposed to explain this, none of them very satisfactory. Perhaps the best is that Matthew may be using this as a device to hint that Jesus did many other such **miracles** for which he has no space in his book. Certainly his emphasis throughout this chapter, and into the next one, is that Jesus is well able to deal with every kind of situation.

But this story carries other meanings as well. After Jesus has quietened the storm, the **disciples** ask one another what sort of a man he can be. Now we get an answer, and from a most surprising source: Jesus, the two demon-possessed men yell out, is 'the **son of God**'! This phrase 'son of God' will later be used by the disciples (14.33), by Peter (16.16), by the chief **priest** (26.63), and by the centurion at the foot of the cross (27.54). It is of course ironic that the first people to address Jesus in this way do so under evil influence, but Matthew would have no doubt that, though the demons are evil and destructive, they have (as it were) access to inside information about spiritual reality.

The best explanation of the phrase 'son of God' here is that it refers to Jesus as **Messiah**. Those who believed in a coming Messiah regarded him as the one who would judge the world and put all wrongs to rights. That is why the demons instantly suspect they are in trouble. If the Messiah is here, the end of their time of freedom has come. They are, in a sense, quite right: Jesus has indeed come to put the forces of evil to flight, and what happens to these demons – entering pigs and driving them into the lake – is a sign of what Jesus will do, in his death and **resurrection**, with all evil of whatever sort.

Everywhere else Jesus went, people asked him to stay with them, and brought him more sick people to cure. Curiously, the people of Gadara regarded him with fear, and begged him to leave their district. Was it because they were Gentiles, and were anxious about the Jewish Messiah coming to them? Was it because they were frightened that if he started sending pigs into the lake he might cause other destruction of property and livestock? We don't know.

What we do know is that wherever Jesus went, people were in awe of him. There was no sense, as in much of the world today, that he was just one teacher among others, one religious leader to be coolly appraised. He was a force to be reckoned with. You might follow him, or you might be scared stiff of him, but you couldn't ignore him. That is the Jesus we must follow today, the Jesus we must make known in the world.

MATTHEW 9.1–8

The Healing of the Paralytic

[1]Jesus got into the boat, and crossed back over to his own town.

[2]Some people brought to him a paralysed man lying on a bed. When Jesus saw their faith, he said to the paralysed man,

'Cheer up, my lad! Your sins are forgiven!'

[3]'This fellow's blaspheming!' said some of the scribes to themselves.

[4]Jesus read their thoughts. 'Why let all this wickedness fester in your hearts?' he said. [5]'Which is easier: to say "Your sins are forgiven", or to say, "Get up and walk?" [6]But, to let you know

that the son of man has authority on earth to forgive sins' – he spoke to the paralysed man – 'Get up, pick up your bed, and go home!'

[7]And he got up, and went away to his home. [8]When the crowds saw it they were frightened, and praised God for giving authority like this to humans.

'Authority' has had a bad press, in much of the world, for a hundred years and more now. It goes together, in the popular mind, with nasty ideas like 'repression', 'human rights abuses', and such like. Think of 'the authorities', and what do you see? Policemen, perhaps. Judges, looking stern and solemn, and ready to send you to prison. Faceless civil servants and bureaucrats, making laws and regulations which seem designed to make life difficult for ordinary people like you.

In some countries, 'the authorities' means something worse still. It means people who knock on your door at five o'clock in the morning, take you away with no good reason, beat you up and maybe kill you. It means people who pass oppressive laws that force you to leave your family for half the year if you want to find any work – or that prevent you from leaving your own town to find work in the next one, because a new border has just been drawn across the map of your own country. 'The authorities' are people who seem to be able to run things the way they want but are answerable to nobody.

What 'authority' really means in all these cases, of course, is 'people who have the power to do what they want'. This usually means 'people who have an army to back them up'. Authority means power, which means force, which means violence. No wonder we're suspicious of the very word 'authority' itself.

Yet here it is again in the **gospel** story: Jesus has authority. You can't miss it. Authority in his teaching. Authority over diseases at a distance. Authority over the storm, over the **demons**. Now, authority to do what normally only God does:

to put away sins, to change a person's life from the inside out, to free them from whatever was gripping them so tightly that they couldn't move. What is this authority? Is it anything like the authorities we know in our world?

Supposing there was a different kind of authority. Supposing there was a different kind of power. A power that didn't work by having an army at its back, and thugs to break down your door at five in the morning; a force that had nothing to do with violence, and everything to do with the strange compelling power of freedom and love. Let's have some of that, you say. Well, that's what's on offer in the gospel.

That's why Jesus' actions were so astonishingly effective – so much so that the people with a little bit of power of their own in his world were angry and upset. That's why Matthew is taking two whole chapters right now to tell us, in one story after another, that this is precisely the sort of authority that Jesus has (see verses 6 and 8). And that's why we need to pay special attention at this point. This is the sort of authority we could all do with.

At the heart of this story is Jesus' claim to forgive sins, to 'put them away' as the Jews often said. The word 'forgive' here literally means 'send away', sending all one's sins off into the far beyond where they are forgotten for ever. That, it seems, is what was needed in this case. In most of Jesus' healings, this wasn't the issue, but it certainly was here.

A glance at the paralysed man on his stretcher told Jesus all he needed to know. This paralysis was the sort where what we would call psychological forces had reduced the body to immoveability. The man had done something – perhaps many things – of which he was deeply ashamed. He was in over his head, as we say, and saw no way out. He not only felt guilty; he *was* guilty, and he knew it. And gradually this gnawing sense of guilt stopped him doing things. Then it stopped him moving his body altogether. And finally his friends took their

faith and their friend in their own hands and brought him to Jesus.

Once again, 'faith' here means 'faith in Jesus' authority'; 'faith that Jesus will be able to do something about it'. That's what Jesus is responding to. He addresses the key problem, knowing that all the symptoms will quickly disappear if the main disease is dealt with. Jesus has no straightforwardly physical means of healing the man. He uses the authority which God has invested in him, authority to forgive sins and so to bring new **life**. He is already acting as 'the **son of man**', the one who is to be enthroned over all the forces of evil (Daniel 7.13–14). He has the right, even in the present, to declare that sin is a beaten foe, and to send it away.

Already in the story we can see, looming up ahead and inviting us forward to the climax of the book, the shape of Jesus' whole ministry. He has come as the son of man, the **Messiah**, Israel's representative. And he has come, not just to deal with the oppression caused by Rome, but to address the deeper and darker oppression caused by evil itself. Beyond that again, he has come to challenge evil's ultimate result, which is not just paralysis but death itself.

That's why, in this story, the language used three times over for what Jesus tells the paralysed man to do would remind Matthew's readers of language they were used to hearing in connection with Jesus' **resurrection**. 'Get up!' he says, and the man got up, 'arose'. When sin is dealt with, resurrection (at whatever level) can't be far behind.

We can also see, embedded in this story, some of the forces that put Jesus on the cross, and thus, unwittingly, contributed to his decisive victory over sin. Those who object to his dramatic and authoritative announcement that the man's sins were put away were no doubt reckoning that this was something only God himself could do. God's normal way of doing it was through the **Temple**-system, through the established and authorized (that word again) priesthood. What they hadn't bargained for was that God would, when the great moment came, delegate this role to 'one like a son of man' through whom authority of the right sort would now be let loose in the world. But the forces of resistance, the forces that see their own power undermined by God's new sort of power, remain angry and obdurate. We shall see in this chapter how they begin to snipe at him and attack him, a process which will grow and swell until Jesus eventually stands before the **high priest** himself and makes, for the last time, a great statement about the authority of the son of man (26.64). After that, all that is left is his death, through which all sins were dealt with – and his own 'getting up', the sign, as in this story, that God was indeed with him, and had given him his own special type of authority, to heal and restore the world.

MATTHEW 9.9–17

The Call of Matthew

⁹As Jesus was walking along, he saw a man called Matthew sitting at the tax-office.

'Follow me!' he said to him. And he rose up and followed him.

¹⁰When he was at home, sitting down to a meal, there were lots of tax-collectors and sinners there who had come to have dinner with Jesus and his disciples. ¹¹When the Pharisees saw it, they said to his disciples,

'Why does your teacher eat with tax-collectors and sinners?'

¹²Jesus heard them.

'It isn't the healthy who need a doctor,' he said, 'it's the sick. ¹³Go and learn what this saying means: "It's mercy I want, not sacrifice." My job isn't to call upright people, but sinners.'

¹⁴Then John's disciples came to him with a question.

'How come,' they asked, 'we and the Pharisees fast a good deal, but your disciples don't fast at all?'

¹⁵'Wedding guests can't fast, can they?' replied Jesus, '– as long as the bridegroom is with them. But sooner or later the bridegroom will be taken away from them. They'll fast then all right.'

¹⁶'No one', he went on, 'sews a patch of unshrunk cloth onto an old coat. The patch will simply pull away from the coat, and you'll have a worse hole than you started with. ¹⁷People don't put new wine into old wineskins, otherwise the skins will split; then the wine will be lost, and the skins will be ruined. They put new wine into new skins, and then both are fine.'

I was a teenager in the famous 1960s. Revolution was in the air. Protests, especially among young people, were the order of the day. Young Americans protested against the Vietnam war. Students in Paris told factory workers they had nothing to lose but their chains (the factory workers mostly ignored them). Undergraduates in Oxford, where I was at the time, protested about almost everything, though the subjects we chose showed how little we really had to grumble about: college food, wearing gowns for lectures, colleges keeping files on student activists.

Looking back a generation later, it seems as though what was really going on was not so much that there were lots of things wrong in the system (though there were some – there always are). Rather, these were the signs that a new generation, that had grown up after the Second World War (1939–45), was no longer happy to be told by its parents to behave in the old ways. It was time to make everything different. Bob Dylan summed it up: 'The times they are a'changing,' he sang. And it really felt like that – however much we may look back now and smile to see how little really did change.

But when Jesus said the times were changing he really meant it, and they really were. That was his answer to the questions and criticisms that bubbled up, not surprisingly, when his movement didn't look what people expected a **kingdom**-movement to look like. This passage is full of questions to which his answer was 'Because everything's different now.'

Why does he eat with tax-collectors and sinners? Because, while other religious leaders of the day saw their task as being to keep themselves in quarantine, away from possible sources of moral and spiritual infection, Jesus saw himself as a doctor who'd come to heal the sick. There's no point in a doctor staying in quarantine. He'll never do his job.

Why do Jesus and his **disciples** not keep the regular fast days which, in Israel in those days, commemorated all the tragic things that had happened in their history – not least the destruction of the **Temple**? Because, while other movements, including that of **John the Baptist**, were waiting for the new day to dawn, Jesus believed that the sun had risen. And, to add another picture to the three he gives, while John the Baptist's movement and the **Pharisees** were lighting candles to remind them of the light of the previous day, before the present darkness, he was opening the curtains to let in the light of the day that he knew was dawning even though they weren't aware of it.

The three pictures Jesus himself gives all show how impossible it is to combine the new thing he's doing with the old way things used to be. You can't combine funerals and weddings: you can't be gloomy while you're celebrating a marriage feast. (At this point a shadow falls across the page; before too long the wedding will be replaced by a funeral, and then there will certainly be room for mourning.) If you're mending an old coat by sticking a patch on it, make sure the patch is made of cloth that's already seasoned and has done all the shrinking it's likely to do. Otherwise, when it shrinks, it will just make the hole worse than it was in the first place. And you can't put new wine into old skins, or there will be an explosion.

We shouldn't, perhaps, try to press the details of each picture for a precise application to the question of Jesus' relation to the Judaism of his day. What the three pictures have in common is Jesus' insistence that the new and the old won't mix. This doesn't mean, of course, that the old was bad. Jesus came, Matthew insists, not to destroy, but to fulfil. It simply means that morning has broken on a new day, God's new day, and the practices that were appropriate for the night-time are now no longer needed.

In the middle of all this newness sits a surprised and grateful man, who centuries of readers have supposed was the writer of this **gospel**. If that is so, we find Matthew, the tax-collector, telling the story of his own calling in the middle of a long list (two chapters in all) of healing **miracles**. Why would he do that?

A moment's thought gives the answer. If you were a tax-collector in the ancient world, or for that matter in the modern one, you would get used to people being angry with you. In Matthew's world it was assumed that tax-collectors could be lumped together with 'sinners', as in verses 10–11. This was because, first, they collaborated with the hated authorities, and, second, because they made extra money for themselves by collecting too much.

Think for a moment what life would have been like for Matthew, day after day and year after year. Suppose it was you. You would sit in your hot little booth, waiting for travellers to pay the toll as they passed from one province into the next. They wouldn't enjoy it and nor would you. Then think what it would be like having a young prophet with a spring in his step and God's kingdom in his heart coming past one day and simply asking you to follow him. Yes: it would feel exactly like a healing miracle. Actually, verse 9 hints at something even more: it would be like a **resurrection**. 'He *arose*,' says the passage literally, using a regular 'resurrection' word, 'and followed him.'

So how could Jesus and his friends not celebrate? They were

in the middle of God's new work, an outpouring of mercy which was already upstaging the Temple itself. As the prophet Hosea (6.6) had seen long ago, what God really wants is mercy, not **sacrifice**. The times were indeed changing. God's new world was being born, and from now on everything would be different. The question for us is whether we are living in that new world ourselves, or whether we keep sneaking back to the old one where we feel more at home.

MATTHEW 9.18–26

The Raising of the Little Girl

[18]As Jesus was saying this, suddenly an official came up and knelt down in front of him.

'It's my daughter!' he said. 'She's just died! But – if you'll come and lay your hand on her, she'll come back to life!'

[19]Jesus got up and followed him. So did his disciples.

[20]Just then a woman appeared. She had suffered from internal bleeding for twelve years. She came up behind Jesus and touched the hem of his coat.

[21]'If I can only touch his coat,' she said to herself, 'I'll be rescued.'

[22]Jesus turned round and saw her.

'Cheer up, young lady!' he said. 'Your faith has rescued you.' And the woman was healed from that moment.

[23]Jesus went into the official's house. There he saw the flute-players, and everybody in a great state of agitation.

[24]'Go away!' he said. 'The little girl isn't dead. She's asleep!' And they laughed at him.

[25]So when everybody had been put out, he went in and took hold of her hand, and she got up. [26]The report of this went out around the whole of that region.

As I write this, Britain's farms are in a state of crisis. A powerful disease has spread through tens of thousands of animals, which have had to be slaughtered. Much of the countryside is closed off; nobody is allowed to walk through fields and woods, or to exercise dogs near where livestock are kept. To gain access to a farming area you have to drive through piles of disinfected straw; if you are on foot, you have to walk through disinfectant. The disease brings horror everywhere it goes, and fear everywhere it might go. Suddenly everyone is taking very strict precautions about animal hygiene, though alas it seems too late.

All societies have hygiene regulations. Often we only notice them when, as in the farms just now, they have to be introduced all of a sudden. But we all learn when to wash our hands, and how to clean cups, plates and cutlery after using them. We don't usually give it a thought. If we did, we'd talk about germs, about infections, about staying healthy.

In societies before modern medicine, where you couldn't cure infections nearly as easily as we can now, it was vital to have strict codes about what you could and couldn't touch, and what to do if you did contract 'impurity'. These weren't silly regulations; they didn't mean you were being 'legalistic'. They were and are practical wisdom to keep society in good shape. The Jewish people, who had plenty of regulations like that in the Bible already, had codified them further to make it clearer to people exactly how to keep from getting sick. And two of the things that were near the top of the list, things to avoid if you wanted to stay 'pure' in that sense, were dead bodies on the one hand, and women with internal bleeding (including menstrual periods) on the other. And in this double story Jesus is touched by a haemorrhaging woman, and then he himself touches a corpse.

No Jew would have missed the point – and Matthew was most likely writing for a largely Jewish audience. In the ordinary course of events, Jesus would have become doubly 'unclean', and would have had to bathe himself and his clothes and wait until the next day before resuming normal social contact. This was quite a usual process. Nobody would have given it much thought, any more than we comment on someone doing the laundry today. But when we read the story from this point of view what actually happened is all the more remarkable.

It all began with a flurry of activity, a man in a panic. He was an 'official' – probably a local civil servant or government agent. Normally such people would keep their dignity; they would walk with a measured tread, and speak calmly to those they met. They had a social status to preserve. But this man has thrown all that out of the window. His little daughter has just died! What can he do? He's heard that there's a prophet in town who seems to be curing people – perhaps he can help! And before he quite knows what he's doing he's rushed out of his house, down the road to where Jesus stands with a crowd of people around him, and he's thrown himself down on the dusty road right there in front of all the neighbours. Who cares about dignity when your daughter's life is at stake?

The story keeps us in suspense while we switch attention from a little girl to an older woman. Having had her particular ailment – internal bleeding – for twelve years, she sees her chance of healing, and takes it. Knowing she was making everyone 'unclean' as she pushes past them, she comes up and touches Jesus.

But at this point we realize that something is different. Her 'uncleanness' doesn't infect him. Something in *him* infects *her*. Jesus turns round, sees her, and tells her, as he told the centurion, that what has made the difference is her own **faith** (8.13; see 9.2, 29). Here is the mystery: Jesus has the power to heal, but those who receive it are those with faith. And the word Matthew uses for 'healing' in verses 21 and 22 is 'save', 'rescue'. No early Christian would miss the point. What Jesus was doing was the beginning of his whole work of rescuing the world, saving the world, from everything that polluted, defaced and destroyed it. And those who would benefit would be those who would believe.

The greatest destroyer is of course death itself. Here we see a stage further in Matthew's description of Jesus' healing work. The official's daughter is already dead, and the people in the house know it. They have already begun the sorrowful process of weeping and wailing, letting their grief have full vent over the lovely young life cut short. Jesus won't have it. Taking a huge risk – they were already laughing at him, and now he was going to go and touch the corpse – he holds the little girl's hand, and she gets up (again the word is a '**resurrection**' word: she 'arose').

We in our modern world have many ways of dealing with personal impurity. Contemporary hygiene and chemicals mean we don't have to worry about it nearly as much as people in the ancient world. But, of course, some of the very chemicals we use, as we now know, pollute our atmosphere, our fields and our crops. Some of our contemporary pressure groups are just as worried about 'pollution' in this environmental sense as the **Pharisees** were with pollution as defined by their purity codes. The followers of Jesus may be called to find ways of dealing with such new pollutions, to explore new types of healing to bring cleansing and a new start to communities, agriculture, and the very air we breathe.

But there are still other types of pollution as well: the pollution which gets into our minds and hearts, into our imagination and memory. How can we get rid of that? One way is to spend time with a story like this. Imagine yourself as an actor or actress in the drama. Suppose you were the official . . . or the woman with the internal bleeding . . . or one of the flute-players in the house . . . or one of the **disciples**, looking on . . .

Or, if you dare, suppose you were . . . Jesus himself . . .

MATTHEW 9.27–37

Jesus' Fame Increases

²⁷As Jesus was leaving the area, two blind men followed him, shouting 'Have pity on us, son of David!' at the tops of their voices.

²⁸Jesus went into the house, and the blind men came to him. 'Do you believe that I can do this?' asked Jesus.

'Yes, Master,' they replied.

²⁹Then Jesus touched their eyes. 'Let it happen for you just as you've believed,' he said. ³⁰And their eyes were opened.

Then Jesus gave them a stern warning. 'Take good care', he said, 'that nobody gets to know about this.' ³¹But they went out and spread the news in the whole of that region.

³²After they had left, people brought to Jesus a demon-possessed man who couldn't speak. ³³Jesus cast out the demon, and the man spoke. The crowds were amazed. 'Nothing like this ever happened in Israel,' they said. ³⁴But the Pharisees said, 'He casts out demons by the prince of demons.'

³⁵Jesus went around all the towns and villages, teaching in their synagogues, announcing the good news of the kingdom, and healing every disease and every sickness. ³⁶When he saw the crowds, he felt deeply sorry for them, because they were distressed and dejected, like sheep without a shepherd. ³⁷Then he said to his disciples, 'There's plenty of harvest to be had, but not many workers! ³⁸So pray the Master of the Harvest to send more workers to harvest his fields!'

For many years now, one of the regular themes of fiction-writers has been the spy story. During the Cold War years in particular, when East and West were deeply suspicious of each other (normally this meant Russia and America, but their respective allies joined in as well), there was a great deal of real-life spying, some of which continues to this day. Double agents work in public for one side and then, when off duty, pass on secrets to the other side. Many thriller-writers have seen their opportunity and written story after story of daring and exciting exploits. Books have turned into movies; movies have made millions; tens of millions of people around the world who never spied for anyone or anything know about James Bond, and have got a whiff of pleasure from the danger and drama of the undercover world, experienced at second or third hand.

At the heart of the strange world of spying is the exciting and threatening idea that people are not what they seem; that those who seem to be on 'our' side may after all be secretly working for 'them'. When people know that secrets are leaking out, everyone is under suspicion: is *he* a traitor? Has *she* been receiving mysterious telephone calls? How did *those two* manage to get so much money in the bank all of a sudden? And, when other rivalries and professional jealousies emerge, it's a wonderful opportunity to cast suspicion on the person you dislike. Start a whispering campaign (*'I don't know for sure, but I think so-and-so may be working for the enemy!'*).

Now move all that back into the first century, and into the Jewish world of ancient Palestine. Who is the enemy? Well, Rome of course; and the self-styled aristocrats who seem to have got all the money; and the people who are collaborating with them. But who is the *real* enemy, behind all that? Ah, you must mean the **satan**, the accuser, the dark power that is out to get us all, out to stop God's work, out to prevent Israel being holy, being upright, being rescued from its present plight. From there it's a short step to asking: Well, then, who around here is secretly working for the satan? And Jesus' opponents saw their chance. Jesus himself is, they said. He's in league with the enemy. He's casting out demons by the prince of demons!

That was, after all, the only explanation they could come up with for why Jesus was so successful – other than believing he was truly from God, which they had no intention of doing. There had been other healers before, but few if any like this.

His own authority, enabling him to tell demons what to do and have them obey him, left onlookers with a stark choice. Either he was God's chosen deliverer: at the very least a great prophet, and perhaps something more. Or he was a spy. He was double-dealing.

Matthew will return to this theme, and give Jesus' answer to it, in chapter 12. But it's important at this point because he has now given us two chapters full of healing **miracles**. And he wants us to see, before Jesus sends the **disciples** out on their own healing mission, just what they were going to be up against. If they say that the leader is a spy, what will they say about his followers (10.25)?

The truly sad thing is that Jesus was anything but in league with the enemy. What he was doing sprang from the deep compassion and sorrow he felt in his own heart and mind as he looked at his fellow-Jews wandering around without anyone giving them the lead they needed. They were like sheep without a shepherd – a regular Old Testament way of describing Israel without a prophet or a king to look after them, to lead them in the right way (e.g. Numbers 27.17; 1 Kings 22.17; Ezekiel 34.5). What he was doing, in his healing of so many – including the two blind men in this passage, and the man possessed of a spirit that made him unable to speak – was beginning to provide that leadership, that new initiative, that Israel needed, and knew it needed. But those who had other agendas, who had themselves hoped to be the standard-bearers for the **kingdom**, were bound to be jealous and react badly. Hence the charge: he's done a deal with the satan. He's a spy. Don't trust him.

Often the only thing you can do when slander like that is being spoken is to carry on doing what you are called to do. Jesus looked at his contemporaries and saw them not only like sheep without a shepherd but, changing the farming imagery, like a field full of wheat with nobody to harvest it. They were eager for God's kingdom, but didn't know where to look to find it. They were ready and waiting for God to act, but who would tell them that this action had already begun?

Outside the Lord's Prayer itself, Jesus doesn't often tell his followers what to pray for, but this time he does. Go to the farmer, he says, and beg him to send workers to bring in the harvest. And, as his followers pray that prayer, the answer comes back worryingly quickly: you are, yourselves, to be the answer to your own prayer. What Jesus has been doing for the last two chapters on his own authority, his followers are now to do at his command. Israel must hear the **message**. Never mind the charges of collusion with the enemy; there's no time to waste.

Where are the fields today ready for harvest? What should our prayer then be? When we can answer that, we may discover, too, how we ourselves might be part of God's answer.

MATTHEW 10.1–15

The Twelve Are Sent Out

¹Jesus called his twelve disciples to him, and gave them authority over unclean spirits, to cast them out and to heal every disease and every sickness.

²These are the names of the twelve apostles. First, Simon, who is called Peter ('the rock'), and Andrew his brother; James the son of Zebedee, and John his brother; ³Philip and Bartholomew, Thomas and Matthew the tax-collector, James son of Alphaeus, and Thaddaeus; ⁴Simon the Cananaean; and Judas Iscariot (who betrayed him).

⁵Jesus sent the Twelve off with these instructions.

'Don't go into Gentile territory,' he said, 'and don't go into a Samaritan town. ⁶Go instead to the lost sheep of the house of Israel. ⁷As you go, declare publicly that the kingdom of heaven is arriving. ⁸Heal the sick, raise the dead, cleanse lepers, cast out demons.

'The message was free when you got it; make sure it's free when you give it. [9]Don't take any gold or silver or copper in your belts; [10]no bag for the road, no second cloak, no sandals, no stick. Workers deserve their pay.

[11]'When you go into a town or village, make careful enquiry for someone who is good and trustworthy, and stay there until you leave. [12]When you go into the house give a solemn greeting. [13]If the house is trustworthy, let your blessing of peace rest upon it, but if not, let it return to you. [14]If anyone won't welcome you or listen to your message, go out of the house or the town and shake the dust off your feet. [15]I'm telling you the truth: it will be more bearable for Sodom and Gomorrah on the day of judgment than for that town.'

'But how will I know the way?' I asked, setting off on my first solo car journey.

'Don't be silly,' said my mother. 'We've been going there for years! You'll know it all right.'

But I didn't. I recognized many parts of the road. But there is all the difference in the world between sitting in a car, while someone else makes the decisions about which road to take, and doing it yourself. I got lost – just five miles from my own home! – and had to backtrack and ask someone for directions, as though I were a stranger in the area.

Up until this moment, Jesus' **disciples** have been passengers in the car, and he's been doing the driving. They have been astonished at what they've seen, but he's made all the decisions, handled all the tricky moments, steered them through the towns and villages, taken the criticisms, and come out in front. Now he's telling them to go off and do it themselves. It doesn't take much imagination to see how they would feel. You want *us* to do it? By *ourselves*?

Matthew takes this opportunity to give us a list of the **Twelve** themselves, calling them for the first time '**apostles**', that is, people who are 'sent out', as Jesus was now sending them, and would later send all those who witnessed his **resurrection**. The number 12 is itself of course full of meaning, as anyone in Jesus' world would recognize; at the heart of what Jesus was up to was his belief that through his work God was at last renewing and restoring Israel, which traditionally had been based upon the twelve tribes. But now the Twelve were not just to be a *sign* that God was restoring Israel; they were to be part of the *means by which* he was doing so.

This is the meaning of the otherwise puzzling verses 5–6. Surely, we ask, Jesus had come for everybody? Didn't he himself say that **Gentiles** would come flooding into the **kingdom** (8.11)? Hasn't Matthew already told us that even at the time of his birth foreign stargazers came to pay him homage (2.1–12)?

Yes, and all of that matters. Jesus will, after his resurrection, reverse these instructions and send the disciples out to all the nations (28.19). But there is an immediate and urgent task, before the wider mission can be built in to the programme. Israel itself must hear the **message**, must be given a chance to repent before it's too late. So far, the Gentiles who have appeared have come at their own initiative; Jesus has not sought them out, and won't do so during his public ministry. If he and his followers had started taking their message to the Gentile world at this stage, no self-respecting Jew would have paid them any more attention. It would have confirmed his enemies' taunts: he was in league with the devil.

But he isn't. He has not come to destroy but to fulfil. Israel's God is indeed the creator God, who loves the whole world and intends to save it, to call the Gentiles as well; but the way he will do that is precisely by fulfilling his promises to Israel. That is Jesus' particular and focused concern, as the later church recognized (e.g. Romans 15.8). The time for the Gentiles will come soon enough. For the moment, every effort must be made to tell the chosen people that their great moment, the fulfilment of their dreams, has arrived.

The instructions Jesus now gives his followers – which must have made them even more nervous, one would imagine – give us a clear idea of what that fulfilment looks like. It doesn't look like the kind of movements and missions Jesus' contemporaries were used to. They aren't to swagger around giving it out that they are the chosen servants of the coming king. They are to be healers, restorers, people who will bring life and hope to others, not grand status to themselves. They are to be scrupulous about avoiding any suggestion that they are on the make, out for money. They mustn't even take cash or provisions with them, or carry the sort of bag that beggars would normally have. They must expect that those who hear and receive their message will feed them; but the **gospel** itself, the all-important message, is free.

The detailed instructions for their arrival in a town must have made them realize just what a responsibility they were carrying. This wasn't a take-it-or-leave-it option. They weren't suggesting to people that there was a new religious experience they could have, a new teaching which might help them with the tricky moral decisions they faced. They weren't even offering people new assurance of God's salvation after their death (though that would come too, in due time). It was more urgent still. God's kingdom was rushing upon them like an express train, and they had to get ready for it.

The healings the disciples were to perform, important as they were for the people concerned, were signs of something more important still: God's new life breaking into the life of Israel, beginning the new day that was dawning with Jesus. If people honoured that message and welcomed it, well and good; if they didn't, solemn actions should be taken to indicate that they had chosen to stay in the night rather than welcome the new morning. There was coming a day, very soon, when those who had chosen Jesus' way of peace would be rescued from a great cataclysm, while those who insisted on the way of violence would wish they had lived instead in – Sodom and Gomorrah! Those towns, down by the Dead Sea, were notorious as the place where God's judgment fell in fire and brimstone (Genesis 19.24–28). Jesus is warning that an even worse fate will befall those who refuse to see God's new day as it dawns, and prefer to stick with the old ways which were leading Israel to ruin.

These instructions were very specific, for a particular situation. But Matthew has recorded them in detail, presumably because he thinks they remain relevant to the church even after Jesus' death and resurrection. How might they apply to the mission of your church, today?

MATTHEW 10.16–23

Sheep among Wolves

[16]'See here,' Jesus continued, 'I'm sending you out like sheep surrounded by wolves. So be as shrewd as snakes, and as innocent as doves.

[17]'Watch out for danger from people around you. They will hand you over to councils, and have you flogged in their synagogues. [18]You will be dragged before governors and kings because of me, as evidence to them and to the nations. [19]But when they hand you over, don't worry how to speak or what to say. What you have to say will be given to you at that moment. [20]It won't be you speaking, you see; it will be the spirit of your father speaking in you.

[21]'One brother will betray another to death; fathers will betray children, and children will rebel against their parents and have them put to death. [22]You will be hated by everyone because of my name. But the one who holds out to the end will be delivered.

[23]'When they persecute you in one town, run off to the next one. I'm telling you the truth: you won't have gone through all the towns of Israel before the son of man comes.'

I went to the fairground with my daughter. We stood in line for over an hour for one of the biggest rides; it looked fun, and everyone was excited and happy to wait for their turn. Finally we boarded the car. Up it went, up and up, higher and higher, and we were eager and ready for it to go as high as possible. But then we got to the top, and both of us squealed in dismay. It was only a hundred feet or so to the bottom, but it looked as though we were about a mile high, and the track ran very nearly vertically downwards. I will never forget that shock, or the way in which we hurtled down the steep ramp, clinging on to each other for dear life.

I have a sense, reading this passage, that the **disciples** must have felt something like that as Jesus' instructions to them turned a corner, from what they were to do to what they were to watch out for. Up till now they had been going along with Jesus. His instructions in the first part of the chapter must have made them feel they were getting higher and higher, but it was all still exciting, and, after all, he was sharing some of his own extraordinary power and authority with them. But now, quite suddenly, they were looking over the edge of a precipice. And they were going to be hurtling down it whether they liked it or not.

Jesus knew, from what had already happened in his public career, that he was running into opposition. It hadn't come as a surprise. He knew well enough that the agendas his contemporaries were following, particularly those who were eager for violent revolution against Rome, were diametrically opposite to the **message** he was advocating. The Sermon on the Mount, as we have seen, was standing received wisdom completely on its head. He can't have been surprised when the **Pharisees** started to mutter that he was in league with the devil. Now he has the difficult task of warning the disciples that it's going to happen to them, too.

Those of us who live in the Western world have become

used to taking it for granted that we live in a tolerant society. We don't expect people to haul us off into court for what we believe. We don't expect to be beaten up because we speak about Jesus. We certainly don't expect to find ourselves coming before governors and monarchs on a charge of treason. But Jesus' message was truly revolutionary, and like all true revolutionaries he and his followers were regarded as very dangerous. The question we face is not so much, 'Isn't it a shame that the rest of the world isn't as tolerant as we are?', but 'Is this a sign that Christianity in the West has somehow compromised itself?'

Whatever we think about that, the story of the early church bears out Jesus' solemn warnings. The disciples were indeed persecuted, beaten, imprisoned and killed. The message of Jesus did indeed divide one family from another, and even split up parents from their children, brothers from brothers and sisters from sisters (Jesus' own brothers and sisters don't seem to have believed in him in his lifetime). But Jesus doesn't think it will take very long for all this to happen. Verse 23 indicates that he sees it all coming very quickly. Though he's sending them out urgently now, the strange event which he refers to as 'the coming of the **son of man**' will happen all too soon, before they have even managed to complete a full tour of all the towns of Israel.

What exactly Jesus (and Matthew) meant by this has been much discussed and puzzled over. Some have thought that it refers to Jesus' 'second coming', or '**parousia**', but, as we shall see with other similar phrases, this is unlikely. The phrase echoes Daniel 7.13, where the 'coming' of 'the son of man' is not his coming from **heaven** to earth, but his coming from earth to heaven: exalted, after suffering, to be the judge and ruler of the world, and particularly of the 'beasts' that have opposed 'the people of the saints of the most high'.

What seems to be meant here is this. The disciples will face the harsh fact of persecution, in which, when called to account for themselves, God will give them special wisdom to make appropriate answer. Families will be divided; they will find themselves chased from town to town; they must hold on and be patient. Eventually the moment will come when God's judgment will fall on those who oppose them; in other words, tragically, on the towns and villages where their message of peace was not accepted. In particular, as we shall see later, it will fall on the capital city, Jerusalem itself, which will reject Jesus and his **gospel**. When that happens, they will be 'rescued' or 'delivered' (verse 22), because this means that 'the son of man' has been vindicated, has 'come' to his father (see 16.27). The end of verse 23 is thus a promise, not simply a warning: continue your mission, because God will vindicate you quickly.

Faced with this awesome challenge, Jesus' sharp advice to his followers was: be shrewd like snakes, but innocent like doves. Christians often find it easy to be one or the other, but seldom both. Without innocence, shrewdness becomes manipulative; without shrewdness, innocence becomes naivety. Though we face different crises and different problems to those of the first disciples, we still need that finely balanced character, reflecting so remarkably that of Jesus himself. If we are in any way to face what he faced, and to share his work, we need to be sure that his own life becomes embodied in ours.

MATTHEW 10.24–31

Warnings and Encouragements

[24]'The disciple isn't greater than the teacher; the slave isn't greater than the master. [25]It's quite enough for the disciple to be like the teacher, and the slave to be like the master. If they called the master of the house 'Beelzebul', think what they're going to call his family!

[26]'Don't be afraid of them. Nothing is hidden, you see, that won't come to light; nothing is secret that won't be made

known. [27]What I tell you in the dark, speak in the light, and what you hear whispered in your ears, announce from the roofs of the houses.

[28]'Don't be afraid of people who can kill the body, but can't kill the soul. The one you should be afraid of is the one who can destroy both body and soul in Gehenna. [29]How much would you get for a couple of sparrows? A penny if you're lucky? And not one of them falls to the ground without your father knowing about it. [30]When it comes to you – why, every hair on your head is counted. [31]So don't be afraid! You're worth much more than a great many sparrows.'

Which command is repeated most often in the Bible?

You might imagine it's something stern: Behave yourself! Smarten up! Say your prayers! Worship God more whole-heartedly! Give more money away!

You'd be wrong. It's the command we find in verses 26, 28 and 31: Don't be afraid.

You can see easily enough why Jesus needed to tell his **disciples** not to be afraid, at this point in his instructions to them. After all, he's warned them that the authorities will be after them; that they will suffer physical and emotional violence; and, now, that people will start calling them the sort of names they have already begun to call him. Plenty to be afraid of there! And yet he says, Don't be afraid.

Why not? What reason does he give?

Not the one we expect. We might imagine that he would say 'because God will look after you'. Well, he does say that, eventually. But the first reason he gives (verses 26–27) is that a time will come when everything will be uncovered. Everything that is presently secret will be made known.

Why should that mean they don't need to be afraid? Lots of people would regard the imminent disclosure of their most private thoughts and words as a further reason to *be* afraid, not as a reason to throw fear to the winds. Jesus seems to be assuming that what will come to light on that day is the disciples' loyalty and **faith**; they will be seen to have followed Israel's true **Messiah**, the world's true Lord. Their patience and perseverance will emerge into the light. What may have looked like obstinacy or even arrogance will at last be seen as what it is, a resolute determination to follow the Lord of life wherever he leads. In other words, truth will out, justice will prevail, and those who have lived with integrity and innocence, despite what the world says about them, will be vindicated. That, rather than a quick God-will-look-after-you message, is what Jesus is ultimately offering.

But if they are to learn not to be afraid, they must also learn that there is one who deserves fear, even though this warning (verse 28) is then balanced again by a further 'don't be afraid' in verse 31. Many people have been puzzled by this passage, and we must look at it a bit more closely. Why would Jesus tell his followers not to be afraid, then to *be* afraid, then *not* to be afraid again, all in the space of a few sentences?

Jesus believed that Israel was faced in his day by enemies at two quite different levels. There were the obvious ones: Rome, Herod, and their underlings. They were the ones who had the power to kill the body. But there were other, darker enemies, who had the power to kill the **soul** as well: enemies who were battling for that soul even now, during Jesus' ministry, and who were using the more obvious enemies as a cover. Actually, it's even worse than that. The demonic powers that are greedy for the soul of God's people are using their very desire for justice and vengeance as the bait on the hook. The people of light are never more at risk than when they are lured into fighting the darkness with more darkness. That is the road straight to the smouldering rubbish-tip, to **Gehenna**, and Jesus wants his followers to be well aware of it. This is what you should be afraid of.

But at the same time, to balance that fear – and indeed to

119

outweigh it altogether – we have one of Jesus' most striking promises about the detailed love and care of God, not only for every one of his creatures, but for every hair on their heads.

It's important to be clear at this point. Some people think that when Jesus urges us to fear the one who can destroy body and soul in **hell**, he is referring to God himself. But the point here is the opposite. God is the one we do *not* have to fear. Indeed, he is the one we can trust with our lives, our souls, our bodies, everything.

I have sometimes heard worthy and serious Christian preachers telling congregations off for imagining that it might be appropriate to pray for quite trivial things: a parking space on a busy street, fine weather for an outdoor event at the church, for some lost article to turn up. Of course, there are far more important things to pray for, and we should be sure we are doing that. But if God really takes note of every single sparrow in the sky, and every single hair of our heads, that means that, just as nothing is too great for him to do, so nothing is too small for him to care about it.

In the present context the **message** is plain. You are worth more than a great many sparrows; so rest assured that God knows and cares about the details of your life, even as you face the temptations and dangers which so easily surround you. Followers of Jesus are bound to expect attacks at all levels. But they should also learn that the one they are serving is stronger than the strongest opponent they will ever meet.

MATTHEW 10.32–42

Jesus Causes Division

[32]'So: everyone who owns up to being on my side, I will own them before my father in heaven. [33]But anyone who disowns me in front of others, I will disown that person before my father in heaven.

³⁴'Don't think it's my job to bring peace on the earth. I didn't come to bring peace – I came to bring a sword! ³⁵I came to divide a man from his father, a daughter from her mother, and a daughter-in-law from her mother-in-law. ³⁶Yes, you'll find your enemies inside your own front door.

³⁷'If you love your father or mother more than me, you won't deserve me. If you love your son or daughter more than me, you won't deserve me. ³⁸Anyone who doesn't pick up their cross and follow after me doesn't deserve me. ³⁹If you find your life you'll lose it, and if you lose your life because of me you'll find it.

⁴⁰'Anyone who welcomes you, welcomes me; and anyone who welcomes me, welcomes the one who sent me. ⁴¹Anyone who welcomes a prophet in the name of a prophet will receive a prophet's reward; and anyone who receives an upright person in the name of an upright person will receive an upright person's reward. ⁴²Anyone who gives even a cup of cold water to one of these little ones, in the name of a disciple – I'm telling you the truth, they won't go short of their reward!'

I was once asked to go and preach at the school which I had attended as a boy. It was one of those annual events that many schools have where we were supposed to remember the great pioneers who had founded the school, developed it, and given it its character.

So that's what I preached about. But I pointed out that something very odd was going on. Each one of the men and women we were honouring had been innovators. They had been the ones who dared to do things differently, to go in a new direction despite the people who wanted to keep things as they were. But we, by reading out a list of their names in a solemn voice, and by holding them up as our founding figures, were in danger of doing the opposite: of saying that we wanted everything to stay just the way it had always been. Do you honour the memory of an innovator by slavishly following what they did, or by daring to be different in your turn?

121

The sermon caused, I think, a mild stir. But it was nothing like the stir which Jesus meant these words to cause. 'Sons against fathers, daughters against mothers' – what on earth could he mean? Rejecting parents and children – not peace on earth, but a sword – can this be Jesus himself? What's going on? How can we get our minds around these strange sayings?

Of course, the New Testament also has a good deal to say about caring for one another within the family. And I know that some have misguidedly taken passages like these as a licence to neglect their own dependants and spend all their time on 'the Lord's work'. But these are stern and uncomfortable words which we can't ignore. They echo down the years into the Christian church of today.

Think of St Francis, leaving his wealthy home despite his father's fury, to go and live a simple life of imitating Jesus as much as he could – and setting an example that thousands still follow today.

Think of those who have faced terrible dangers for the sake of the **gospel** and have had to send their families to a place of safety elsewhere, while they have stayed to look after a church because there wasn't anyone else to do it.

Jesus doesn't say here that everyone who follows him will find themselves split off from their families; certainly not. Indeed, many of the **apostles**, in the days of the early church, took their spouses with them on their travels (1 Corinthians 9.5). But Jesus is once again talking about priorities, and is making remarkable and quite drastic claims.

He isn't saying (as some have tried to pretend that he was saying) that what matters is following God in your own way. He is saying, loud and clear, that what matters is allegiance to him: allegiance to Jesus must come at the top of every priority list. We can see, as the story unwinds, how difficult this was even for those who knew him personally: Peter denied him, Judas betrayed him, the rest all ran away and hid. But the challenge remains, embracing everything, demanding everything, offering everything, promising everything.

The absolute demand of Jesus brings us back to where we were in the Sermon on the Mount. It isn't the case that there are some fine ideals in the mind of God, and that Jesus just happens to teach them a bit better than most people. Nor is it the case that Jesus came to show the way through the present world to a quite different one, where we will go after death. No: Jesus came to begin and establish *the new way of being God's people*, and not surprisingly those who were quite happy with the old one, thank you very much, didn't like having it disturbed. He didn't want to bring division within households for the sake of it. But he knew that, if people followed his way, division was bound to follow.

Actually, the passage about sons and fathers, daughters and mothers, and so on, is a quotation from one of the Old Testament prophets (Micah 7.6). In this passage, the prophet predicts the terrible divisions that would always occur when God was doing a new thing. When God acts to rescue his people, there are always some who declare that they don't need rescuing, that they are comfortable as they are. Part of the reason for quoting this passage here is to say: don't be surprised if this happens now; this, too, is part of your tradition! Your own scriptures contain warnings about the great disruptions that will happen when God finally acts once and for all to save you.

That's why Jesus' challenge, to the **disciples** themselves and, through them, to the Israel of his day, had to be so sharp – and often has to be just as sharp today, where people still naturally prefer comfort to challenge. But the challenge of Jesus' sayings is matched by the remarkable promises he makes to those who accept them and live by them. He will 'own' us before his father in **heaven**. Those who lose their lives will find them. And, at the end, the remarkable chain reaction of those who serve their fellow human beings out of love for Jesus. Give a cup of cold water to one of Jesus' least significant followers, and you're giving it to Jesus himself; whatever you do for Jesus, you do, not just for Jesus, but for God ('the one who sent me'). If Jesus' people today could relearn this simple but profound lesson, the church might once again be able to go out with a message to challenge and change people's hearts.

MATTHEW 11.1–6

Jesus and John the Baptist

¹So when Jesus had finished giving instructions to the twelve disciples, he went away from there to teach and preach in their towns.

²Meanwhile, John, who was in prison, heard about these messianic goings-on. He sent word through his own followers.

³'Are you the one who is coming?' he asked. 'Or should we be looking for someone else?'

⁴'Go and tell John', replied Jesus, 'what you've seen and heard. ⁵Blind people are seeing! Lame people are walking! Lepers are being cleansed! Deaf people can hear again! The dead are being raised to life! And – the poor are hearing the good news! ⁶And God bless you if you're not upset by what I'm doing.'

We had rehearsed the show for weeks, and reckoned we had it pretty well sorted out. We were a bunch of enthusiastic amateurs, but we were quite pleased with our singing, acting and dancing. The show was going to be good, funny and exciting. People would love it. And they did.

But in the last performance, the star of the show had a new idea. He didn't tell anyone. He simply, at a crucial moment, did the opposite of what we'd rehearsed. He had realized we were in danger of getting stale, and knew that if he shocked us on stage our reactions would be all the better. He was right. We all jumped like startled rabbits, just as if we'd been practising the move for ages. The audience loved it. We all responded, and the performance became electric. It wasn't what we'd expected, but it was better than we'd dared to hope.

Throughout this chapter Jesus is dealing with the fact that what he's doing is not what people were expecting him to. He knows it, is facing it, and believes that this is the way to go, the way to bring in God's **kingdom** even though this isn't what others had imagined. The trouble is, though, that in terms of the illustration the other actors aren't necessarily getting the message, and the audience is getting puzzled. Later in the chapter, we'll see how the people in his own town of Capernaum were getting the wrong idea and refusing to go along with his new interpretation of what God's kingdom would be like. But we begin with something that must have been even harder for Jesus to bear. His own cousin and colleague was having doubts. Had Jesus forgotten the script? Hadn't he remembered what he was supposed to be doing?

John, we recall, was in prison; Matthew has already mentioned this (4.12), and will tell the story more fully in 14.3–12. King Herod had taken exception to John's fiery preaching, and particularly to his denunciation of him for marrying his brother's ex-wife. This was all part of John's announcement that God's kingdom – and God's true king – were on the way. Herod wasn't the real king; God would replace him. No wonder Herod put him in prison.

But now, in prison, John was disappointed. He heard about what Jesus was doing, and it didn't sound at all like the show he thought they'd rehearsed. He was expecting Jesus to be a man of fire, an Elijah-like character who would sweep through Israel as Elijah had dealt with the prophets of Baal (the pagan god many Israelites worshipped instead of YHWH). No doubt John looked forward eagerly to the day, not long now, when Jesus would confront Herod himself, topple him from his throne, become king in his place – and get his cousin out of prison, and give him a place of honour.

125

But it seemed as though Jesus was working to a different script altogether. (Matthew refers to what Jesus was doing as 'his messianic deeds', but part of the point is that John didn't see them like that.) Jesus was going around befriending tax-collectors and 'sinners' (people whom strict Jews would regard as outsiders, not keeping the **Torah** properly). He was gaining a great reputation – but not for doing what John wanted him to do. What was going on? Had John been mistaken? Was Jesus after all 'the one who was to come' – the one the play demanded, the one written into the script John thought they were acting out?

Yes and no. Jesus believed – and Matthew wants us to get this clear – that he really was 'the one who was to come'. He really was the **Messiah**. But he had rewritten the key bit of the play, to the surprise and consternation of the other actors and the audience as well. He was going back to a different script, a different kind of story.

He wasn't thinking of himself in terms of Elijah calling down fire from **heaven**. He was thinking of passages like Isaiah 35, the great prophecies of what would happen when Israel was not so much judged and condemned, but restored *after* judgment. **Exile** would be over, the blind and the lame would be healed, God's people would be set free at last.

Jesus is actually one jump ahead, in the story-line, of where John thinks he should be. John wants him to bring judgment – and so, in a sense, he will. But already the mercy which comes after judgment, the healing which comes after the time of sorrow, is breaking in, and it's Jesus' job to bring it. This, according to Jesus (and Matthew), is the Messiah's main task.

Actually, Jesus wasn't the only one at the time who thought the Messiah would do things like this. In one of the **Dead Sea Scrolls** found at Qumran there's a passage which predicts that when the Messiah comes he will heal the sick, raise the dead, bring **good news** to the poor, and so on. The difference is that

126

Jesus was actually *doing* these things. Just as wicked people don't like the message of judgment, because they think (rightly) that it's aimed at them, so sometimes good people don't like the message of mercy, because they think (wrongly) that people are going to get away with wickedness.

But mercy was at the heart of Jesus' messianic mission, just as it remains at the heart of the church's work today. Whether or not that's the script people want us to follow, that's the way we've got to go. And Jesus invokes a special blessing on people who realize that this is the true story – which turns into a coded warning to those who are puzzled, including poor John himself. This is where and how God is at work. Those who recognize it, and are not offended because they were expecting something else, will know God's blessing.

MATTHEW 11.7–15

The Identity of John the Baptist

[7]As the messengers were going away, Jesus began to speak to the crowds about John.

'What were you expecting to see,' he asked, 'when you went out into the desert? A reed wobbling in the wind? [8]No? Well, then, what were you expecting to see? Someone dressed in silks and satins? If you want to see people like that you'd have to go to somebody's royal palace. [9]All right, so what *were* you expecting to see? A prophet? Ah, now we're getting there: yes indeed, and much more than a prophet! [10]This is the one the Bible was talking about when it says,

See, I'm sending my messenger ahead of you
And he will clear your path before you.

[11]'I'm telling you the truth: John the Baptist is the greatest mother's son there ever was. But even the least significant person in heaven's kingdom is greater than he is. [12]From the

127

time of John the Baptist until now the kingdom of heaven has been forcing its way in – and the men of force are trying to grab it! ¹³All the prophets and the law, you see, make their prophecies up to the time of John. ¹⁴In fact, if you'll believe it, he is Elijah, the one who was to come. ¹⁵If you've got ears, then listen!'

One of the things that made the start of the twentieth century so dramatic was the invention of the motor car. It brought all kinds of new opportunities, new dangers, and new possibilities. But think for a moment of just one of the great changes that came about because of it.

Imagine you have worked all your life in a family-based company making something people have always wanted for centuries, and as far as you have known will always go on wanting: horse-drawn carriages. You're good at it. One brother is excellent at designing new models. Another supervises the small and devoted workforce. A cousin travels around taking orders and making sure previous customers are still happy.

Then one day another brother comes into the office. He's been talking to the business world about the way things are going. His words carry good news for many, but bad news for the family firm.

'Look at it like this,' he says. 'You three are the greatest carriage-makers in the country. You draw them, you build them, you sell them, better than anyone else! Nobody can touch you! But the news is this: *we aren't going to be making carriages much longer.* From now on, the junior mechanic making motor cars in a factory is going to be doing better than you.'

Far be it from me to suggest that the invention of the motor car, and all that has gone with it, has anything much to do with the coming of the **kingdom of God**. Cars have been a blessing and a curse in at least equal measure. But the point is this: Jesus was paying **John the Baptist** a very great compliment, *but*

saying that the time for that sort of work had come to an end.
The kingdom of heaven was now breaking in – remember how,
in 4.12, Jesus began to announce the presence of the kingdom
precisely when John was put in prison – and the whole sweep
and swathe of history that led up to John and his work was
now being wound up. Not because it was a failure, but because
it was a success (here the carriage/car picture doesn't help so
much). If the **law** and the prophets were looking forward to
something that was yet to come, they are set aside when the
new thing arrives, not because they haven't told the truth but
because they have.

The point of all this is that Jesus is offering a new way of
understanding God's timetable. In a few simple words, he is
telling his hearers that Israel's long history, from Abraham
and Moses through the prophets to the present moment, was
one long preparation, one long getting-ready time. Now the
preparation was over, and the reality had dawned. John was
indeed the greatest among the preparers, but even the most
insignificant person who was accepting God's kingdom and
living by it – in other words, who was hearing Jesus and following him – was 'greater', simply because they were living in
the time of fulfilment.

In other words, says Jesus, John was 'Elijah – the one who was
to come.' Jesus here echoes what John had said in his question
in verse 3: 'Are you the one who is to come?' Maybe what Jesus
is saying, or at least hinting, is, 'No – that's you! *You're* the man
of fire, the Elijah-person; I'm the one who comes *after* the
Elijah-person.' This is only a hint; that's why he tells his hearers
to 'listen – if you've got ears!' That's the sort of thing you add
if you have said something a bit cryptic, something which you
don't want to spell out any further but want people to work
out for themselves.

But why? Why would Jesus want to say this, and why would
he be anxious not to say it too clearly?

The answer is lurking underneath the earlier part of the passage, and again it's cryptic. Its meaning only really emerges when you stop and think. Who had put John in prison? Herod Antipas. Who did Herod think he was? King of the Jews. Who did John hope Jesus might be? The **Messiah**, the true king of the Jews. What would have happened if Herod had heard that there was a rival king of the Jews on the loose? Another prisoner . . . and perhaps another dead prisoner.

So Jesus refuses to come out and say, in public, 'Yes, I'm the Messiah.' He is doing messianic things (the healings), and he will do more. He is teaching on his own authority. He has chosen twelve **disciples**, symbolizing Israel's renewal, and has sent them off on a mission to tell the whole country about him and his kingdom-movement. But he isn't going to let word get back to Herod's palace that he is claiming to be king.

Instead, he teases the crowds into thinking harder about who John was – and who, therefore, Jesus himself must be. John wasn't like the royalty they knew. He was nothing like Herod (whose emblem, on his coins, was a Galilean reed waving in the wind). He wasn't dressed in the sort of fine clothes that rich and famous people, especially royalty, would wear. John was different: he was a prophet. Not just any old prophet, either, but the prophet that previous prophets had spoken about: he was the one destined to get the path ready for God's Messiah to walk along when he arrived.

The point is this: Jesus isn't just telling the crowds about John. He's telling them about himself – but doing so obliquely. To come out and declare his own messiahship would be both dangerous and, in a strange way, all wrong. Precisely because of the sort of Messiah Jesus is trying to be, he doesn't want to force himself on people. They have to work it out for themselves.

That is just as true today as ever it was. If we, as Christians, go around simply telling people that we're God's people, that we are Jesus' followers and representatives, they may not be very impressed. We may run into all sorts of difficulties. Far better that they get to hear, like John in prison, 'the messianic goings-on', and ask what's happening. Far better that we explain ourselves in such a way that forces them to think it all out for themselves.

MATTHEW 11.16–24

Jesus Condemns the Cities

[16]'What picture shall I give you for this generation?' asked Jesus. 'It's like a bunch of children sitting in the town square, and singing songs to each other. [17]This is how it goes:

> You didn't dance when we played the flute,
> You didn't cry when we sang the dirge!

[18]'What do I mean? When John appeared, he didn't have any normal food or drink – and people said "What's got into him, then?" [19]Then along comes the son of man, eating and drinking normally, and people say, "Ooh, look at him – guzzling and boozing, hanging around with tax-collectors and the riff-raff." But, you know, wisdom is as wisdom does – and wisdom will be vindicated!'

[20]Then he began to berate the towns where he'd done most of his powerful deeds, because they hadn't repented.

[21]'It's a bad day for you, Chorazin!' he said. 'It's a bad day for you, Bethsaida! If Tyre and Sidon had seen the kind of powerful things you saw, they would have repented long ago with hairshirts and ashes. [22]But I can tell you this: on the day of judgment Tyre and Sidon will have a better time of it than you will. [23]And what about you, Capernaum? You think you're going to be exalted to heaven, do you? No – you'll be sent down to Hades! If the powerful works that happened in you had happened in Sodom, it would still be standing today. [24]But I can tell you this: on the day of judgment the land of Sodom will have a better time of it than you will!'

A bright red sports car swept by me in the street, with a roar of exhaust and a swish of tyres. As it slowed momentarily to take the corner, I caught a glimpse of the young man driving it: dark glasses, long hair, the hint of a beard. Rock music was playing at full blast on the car's stereo. The sticker in the back window of the car said: 'I'M THE ONE YOUR MOTHER WARNED YOU ABOUT.' He was clearly proud of the fact.

Most societies have warned children about certain types of people, and the ancient Israelites were no exception. In the book called Deuteronomy, which sets out the commands and warnings given by Moses to the children of Israel immediately before they crossed the river to take possession of the promised land, there are clear warnings about certain types of persons and what they may do.

Beware of false prophets, said Moses; they will try to lead you astray from following YHWH, and you must resist them. Beware of a rebellious son, he said, one who refuses to obey his parents. He will bring evil upon Israel, and his parents must bring him to the elders of the town and have them put him to death.

This harsh commandment (Deuteronomy 21.18–21) instructs the parents of such a son to accuse him in a particular way. 'This son of ours', they must say, 'is stubborn and rebellious. He will not obey us. He is a glutton and a drunkard.' Then the people must stone him to death.

But where have we heard this sort of thing before?

In this passage – on the lips of Jesus himself. This, it seems, is what people are saying about him: he's a guzzler and a boozer, a glutton and a drunkard, he likes his parties and his food and drink. *He must be a rebellious son, leading Israel astray*! Maybe he's a false prophet as well. This charge surfaces again later in the book.

Jesus was up against it, and clearly found it frustrating. **John the Baptist** had led a life of self-denial, like the holy ascetics in many traditions. Ordinary people had found that hard to take. They had even suspected that a **demon** might have got into him. Now here was Jesus himself, celebrating the **kingdom of heaven** with all and sundry, throwing parties which spoke of God's lavish, generous love and forgiveness – and people accused him of being a rebel, a son who wouldn't behave, a false prophet! The answer, of course, then as now, is that people don't like the challenge, either of someone who points them to a different sort of life entirely, or of someone who shows that God's love is breaking into the world in a new way, like a fresh breeze blowing through a garden and shaking old blossom off the trees.

And they certainly didn't like it when this meant Jesus challenging them to turn away from the direction they'd been going and take the opposite path instead. Some of Jesus' sternest warnings are reserved, as in verses 20–24, for those who refuse this call. Why? What was going on? Was he just angry, and calling down a curse on them?

No. These warnings are among the most sober and serious words he ever said. He had lived in Capernaum, after all; he knew the people. They were his friends, his neighbours. The baker where he bought his bread. The people he met in the synagogue. And he knew Chorazin and Bethsaida, just a short walk along the lakeside. And he knew now, despite all the remarkable things he'd done there, that they were bent on going their own way, following their own vision of God's kingdom. And he knew where that would lead.

Their vision of the kingdom was all about revolution. Swords, spears, surprise attacks; some hurt, some killed, winning in the end. Violence to defeat violence. A holy war against the unholy warriors. Love your neighbour, hate your enemy; if he slaps you on the cheek, or makes you walk a mile with him, stab him with his own dagger. That's the sort of kingdom-vision they had. And Jesus could see, with the clarity both of the prophet and of sheer common sense, where it would lead. Better be in Sodom and Gomorrah, with fire and brimstone raining from **heaven**, than fighting God's battles with the devil's weapons.

He was offering a last chance to embrace a different kingdom-vision. He'd outlined it in his great sermon and the teaching he was giving in towns and villages all over Galilee. He was living it out on the street, and in houses filled with laughter and friendship. He was showing how powerful it was with his healings. And they didn't want it – and were ready to use any excuse ('He's got a demon!' 'He's a guzzler and boozer!' 'He's the one they warned us about!') to avoid the issue.

What are the excuses people use today to avoid the issue of the kingdom? What is likely to happen as a result? How can we continue to live and teach God's kingdom in a world that basically doesn't want to know?

MATTHEW 11.25–30

Jesus' Invitation

^{25}At that time Jesus turned to God with this prayer:

'I give you my praise, father, master of heaven and earth! You hid these things from the wise and intelligent and revealed them to children! ^{26}Yes, father, that's the way you decided to do it! ^{27}My father gave me everything: nobody knows the son except the father, and nobody knows the father except the son – and anyone the son wants to reveal him to.

^{28}'Are you having a real struggle? Come to me! Are you carrying a big load on your back? Come to me – I'll give you a rest! ^{29}Pick up my yoke and put it on; take lessons from me, I'll be gentle with you! The last thing in my heart is to give you a hard time. You'll see – rest you need, and rest you shall have. ^{30}My yoke is easy to wear, my load is easy to bear.'

I went this morning to a memorial service to honour one of

the world's great sportsmen. Colin Cowdrey was one of the greatest cricketers of all time; not quite cricket's Babe Ruth, but not far off. He was known and loved all around the world – not least in India, Australia, Pakistan and the West Indies, whose cricketers had learned to fear and respect his extraordinary ability, and whose crowds had come to love him as a man, not just as a player.

The service was magnificent. Tributes flowed in from around the world; a former prime minister gave the main address; a special song had been written. But for me the most moving moment was when one of Cowdrey's sons came forward and spoke of his father from his inside knowledge. This great public figure, who gave of himself in later life to every good cause he could find, had never lost his close and intimate love for his children and grandchildren. There were many fine stories which only a son could know, and only a son could tell. It was a heartwarming and uplifting occasion.

This remarkable passage in Matthew shows Jesus coming to the same recognition about the one he called 'father'. There were things about his father that, for some reason, only he seemed to know, and only he could tell.

There is a deep mystery here which takes us right to the heart of what it meant to be Jesus. As he announced God's **kingdom** and put God's powerful love to work in healing, forgiving and bringing new life, he obviously realized that the other people he met, including the religious leaders, his own followers, and the ordinary people, didn't have the same awareness of his father that he did.

Imagine a gifted musician walking around among people who can only just manage to sing in tune. That must have been what it was like for Jesus. He must have known from early on that there was something different about him, that he seemed to have an inside track on knowing who Israel's God truly was, and what he was wanting for his people.

This must have made it all the more galling when he discovered that most of his contemporaries didn't want to hear what he was telling them. Most of them, alarmed at the direct challenge he presented, were either resisting him outright or, as we've seen, making excuses for not believing him or following him. Opposition was mounting. And, strangely, this gave Jesus a fresh, further insight into the way his father was operating. This, in turn, resulted in a burst of praise as he glimpsed the strange, unexpected way God was working.

Jewish writings had, for a millennium and more, spoken warmly about the wisdom of the wise. God gave wisdom to those who feared him; a long tradition of **Torah**-study and piety indicated that those who devoted themselves to learning the law and trying to tease out its finer points would become wise, would ultimately know God. For the average Jew of Jesus' day, this put 'wisdom' about as far out of reach as being a brain surgeon or test pilot seems for most people today. You needed to be a scholar, trained in languages and literature, with leisure to ponder and discuss weighty and complicated matters.

Jesus sliced through all that with a stroke. No, he declared: you just need to be a little child. Jesus had come to know his father the way a son does: not by studying books about him, but by living in his presence, listening for his voice, and learning from him as an apprentice does from a master, by watching and imitating. And he was now discovering that the wise and learned were getting nowhere, and that the 'little people' – the poor, the sinners, the tax-collectors, ordinary folk – were discovering more of God, simply by following him, Jesus, than the learned specialists who declared that what he was doing didn't fit with their complicated theories.

As a result, Jesus had come to see that he was himself acting as a window onto the living God. Where he was, and through his words, people were coming to see who 'the father' really was.

He seemed to have the gift and the task of drawing back the curtain and 'unveiling' the truth about God; and the word for 'unveil' here is *apocalypse*, which still today speaks of something dramatic, sudden and earth-shattering.

Wasn't that a bit daunting for his followers? Isn't it rather forbidding to discover that the true God can be known only through Jesus? No. It might have felt like that if it had been somebody else; but with Jesus everything was different. It gave him the platform from which to issue what is still the most welcoming and encouraging invitation ever offered. 'Come to me,' he said, 'and I'll give you rest.' The **Pharisees** had spoken of people being called to carry 'the yoke of the Torah', the heavy burden of the Jewish law with all its commandments. Jesus offered a different 'yoke', which, because it came from his mercy and love, was easy to bear.

How could following Jesus really be that easy? Didn't he say, himself, that people had to be prepared to leave behind family, possessions, even their own life? Yes, he did. But the ease and the joy, the rest and the refreshment which he offered, all spring from his own inner character, his gentleness and warmth to all who turn to him, weighed down by burdens moral, physical, emotional, financial or whatever. He is offering what he has in himself to offer.

When he declares here, in the old translation, that he is 'meek and lowly of heart', he isn't boasting that he's attained some special level of spiritual achievement. He is encouraging us to believe that he isn't going to stand over us like a policeman, isn't going to be cross with us like an angry schoolteacher. And the welcome he offers, for all who abandon themselves to his mercy, is the welcome God offers through him. This is the invitation which pulls back the curtain and lets us see who 'the father' really is – and encourages us to come into his loving, welcoming presence.

MATTHEW 12.1–14

Lord of the Sabbath

[1]At that time Jesus went through the cornfields on the sabbath. His disciples were hungry, and they began to pluck ears of corn and eat them. [2]When the Pharisees observed this they said to him,

'Look here! Your disciples are doing something that's not permitted on the sabbath!'

[3]'Did you never read what David did?' replied Jesus. 'When he and his men were hungry, [4]they went into God's house and ate the holy bread which neither he nor his men were allowed to eat – only the priests had that right. [5]Or didn't you read in the law that the priests in the Temple do things on the sabbath which are against sabbath law – and they aren't guilty? [6]Let me tell you this: something greater than the Temple is here. [7]If you'd known what this saying means:

Mercy, not sacrifice, is what I really want –

you wouldn't have passed judgment on blameless people. [8]Yes, you see: the son of man is master of the sabbath, too.'

[9]He left the place and went into their synagogue, [10]where there was a man with a withered hand.

They put the question to him: 'Is it lawful to heal on the sabbath?'

(They asked this so that they could frame a charge against him.)

[11]'Supposing one of you has a sheep,' replied Jesus, 'and it falls into a ditch on the sabbath. You'll grab it and haul it out, won't you? [12]Well then, think how much more important a human being is than a sheep! So, you see, it is permitted to do good on the sabbath.'

[13]Then he said to the man, 'Stretch your hand out.' He stretched it out, and it was restored to health, just like the other one. [14]But the Pharisees went off and plottted against him, with the intention of doing away with him.

138

Some years ago I read a book by a man who had worked most of his life with poor and homeless people in one of the toughest parts of London. It was a gritty tale of just how hard real life can be for some people – and of how the love of God can come into the middle of the squalor and sadness and change things for the better. At the heart of it, the writer stressed again and again that, despite the values of the society all around, which was prepared to leave people on the scrap-heap provided their own material comfort and affluence was assured, he believed that God cared more for a single human being than for all the trappings of wealth and fortune. The title of his book summed all this up in a well-known phrase: *People Matter More Than Things.*

This passage, with two stories of Jesus being challenged about what he and his **disciples** were doing on the **sabbath**, could be entitled, 'People matter more than sheep.' Of course, sheep do matter; Jesus said, a couple of chapters ago, that God knows about every fallen sparrow. But people matter much, much more. And that's the lever that Jesus used to get underneath the hardened prejudices of his contemporaries and overturn them.

Let's be clear about this. Jesus wasn't saying the sabbath was a bad idea, or that God had changed his mind from the time when he insisted on people observing it, even sometimes on pain of death. He was attacking the way it had become so powerful a system that the people who were agitating for it to be observed strictly had forgotten whose **law** it was, or what such laws were supposed to be all about. They were there to ensure that God's love for his people would not be interrupted by people being over-eager to work more than they should. But if the law, strictly applied, was getting in the way of that love, as it flowed out to reach and heal people in desperate need, then it was the law that was wrong. People matter more than things, even when the 'things' are part of the biblical law.

And Jesus, remarkably, claimed to have authority over it. 'The son of man is master of the sabbath, too' (12.8)! The phrase '**son of man**' here seems to refer to Jesus as the one who (as in earlier chapters) is carrying God's authority. It ties in these sayings and actions to the wider story of all that he is doing, all that leads to the final clash with the authorities and then to his death.

That final clash, in fact, is hinted at in the first of the two short stories. When the **Pharisees**, like first-century investigative journalists on the trail of a politician they want to do down, ask Jesus about the behaviour of his followers, Jesus doesn't take the easy way out of explaining that they were hungry, and that maybe human hunger overrides sabbath law. He raises the stakes much higher, talking of something King David did in God's house. This isn't just an ancient biblical example of how someone got around a law. It's a much more powerful, and much more dangerous, story for Jesus to line himself up with. This time, it isn't just that people matter more than things; it's that Jesus and his followers matter more than the **Temple**.

At the time of the story in question (1 Samuel 21.1–6), David had already been anointed as king by the prophet Samuel, but Saul was still the actual king. David was on the run, escaping from Saul who, not surprisingly, wanted to get rid of him. When David and his followers arrived at the house of God in Shiloh (this was, of course, before the Temple in Jerusalem had been built), they were given the special, holy bread to eat that normally only the **priests** would be able to touch. Clearly the priests in question were quietly supporting David's royal claim.

When Jesus quoted this story to explain what he and his disciples were doing, he was saying two things, both of which explain the anger he aroused. First, he is the true king; like David, he has been anointed, but not yet enthroned. (A good part of the **gospel** story is a matter of explaining how he moves

140

from the 'anointing' at his **baptism** to the 'enthronement' on the cross.) Second, he and his followers are more important than the Temple itself; not just because people matter more than things, but because Jesus matters more than Solomon's Temple and all that goes on in it.

This is fighting talk, both for the self-appointed guardians of tradition, the Pharisees, and for any priests to whom this extraordinary claim might get back. When Jesus finally arrives in Jerusalem, these same things – his royal claim, and his attitude to the Temple – are what get him arrested, tried and killed. Matthew wants us to see the shadow of the cross already falling over the story.

What systems are currently in danger of being exalted over the needs of real human beings, in your country, your church, your family? What would it mean for the son of man to be master of them?

MATTHEW 12.15–21

The Servant

[15]Jesus discovered the plots against him, and left the district. Large crowds followed him, and he healed them all, [16]giving them strict instructions not to tell people about him. [17]This was so that what was spoken through Isaiah the prophet might come true:

> [18]Look! Here's my servant, whom I chose;
> My beloved one, my heart's delight.
> My spirit I will place on him,
> And he'll announce my justice
> To the whole wide world.
> [19]He will not argue, nor will he
> Lift up his voice and shout aloud;
> Nobody in the streets will hear
> His voice. [20]He will not break the damaged

Reed, or snuff the guttering lamp,
Until his judgment wins the day.
²¹The world will hope upon his name.

The bishop sat at his desk and put his head in his hands. Another three letters had just arrived complaining at the way in which a particular parish had changed its style of music. The director of finance had just reported that unless people in the diocese gave a lot more money in the next six months they would have to close some churches and make two or three priests redundant. The police were investigating a church worker following some serious allegations. One of his closest colleagues had just had a major operation and was beginning two months' sick leave. And now a telephone call had informed him that one of his own children was in trouble at school and he must come at once.

As he paused, his head spinning with all the bad news, there came into his mind the verse he'd heard at morning prayer an hour or so before. 'The world will hope upon his name.' Matthew, quoting Isaiah.

From somewhere – it seemed a long way away – he could see in his mind's eye an African village, where a young catechist was explaining to an eager group what it meant to follow Jesus' costly **kingdom**-way rather than to jump on the bandwagon of popular revolutionary movements. He saw, behind them, the hospital they had already built, the wells they had dug. Then he saw a huge congregation in Latin America, celebrating God's love in the middle of poverty and despair. He saw the dwindling churches of the Middle East, surrounded by hostile governments and religious pressure groups, facing problems nobody in the Western world could even imagine. He saw the faces of a young Pakistani couple he'd visited a few months previously, bringing their first child for **baptism** in a village church some miles outside Karachi. And, finally, he saw the teenagers he had confirmed the previous evening in a parish in his own diocese. These stories, he thought, are all telling The Story. The story of one man, one name, one hope, one world. Somehow the letters and the telephone calls and the worrying reports are part of that Story as well. Somehow they belong.

And he felt, perhaps, something of what Matthew was trying to tell us in this passage. Here is Jesus, surrounded by pressures on all sides. His own followers don't yet really understand what he's doing. People are badgering him from every direction to heal them, to cast out evil spirits, to be there for them in their every need. At the same time, opposition is growing. Herod is not far away. Religious pressure groups are stirring up trouble. Some are even saying he's in league with the devil. He knows where it's all leading. And still he goes on.

And he goes on because he has a story in mind. The story of the Servant: Isaiah's story, the most famous story of the most famous prophet. The story of the Servant begins in the passage Matthew quotes here; it's taken from Isaiah 42. The 'Servant of **YHWH**' is a strange figure in Isaiah: one who will bring YHWH's blessing and justice to the world – the task which, earlier in Isaiah, was assigned to the **Messiah**, the coming king. But how is the Servant to accomplish his task? Not, it seems, by bullying and harrying Israel and the nations, by threatening and fighting. Rather, with a quiet and gentle work of healing, bearing the love and grace of God to the dark parts of Israel and the world.

Matthew looks back over the ministry of Jesus, knowing where it would lead. He sees Jesus as the Servant, not only when he dies a cruel death, wounded for our transgressions and bruised for our iniquities, but also in the *style* of what he was already doing in Galilee. He was going about bringing God's restoration wherever it was needed, not by making a fuss, but by gently leading people into God's healing love.

This is the story of one 'in whose name the nations will hope'. Well, they would, wouldn't they?

The nations – and, alas, Israel as well, as becomes clear in Matthew's story – are bent on violence and arrogance. Those who want peace and who work for it are always, in the end, shouted down by those who want more money, more land, more security, more status, and are prepared to fight and kill to get it. Those who are great and mighty in this world's terms make sure their voices are heard in the streets. Those who shout loudest get obeyed the soonest. But that's not the Servant's way.

So, too, those who want to get ahead in this world tend to push others out of the way. If they see a weak link – a rod that's bent and could break, a candle that's almost gone out – they will trample on it without a thought. That's not the Servant's way. The nations are used to arrogance. Here is a Servant who is the very opposite. He is the one shining light, the one hopeful sign.

And if the nations can hope in him, then hard-worked and hard-pressed church workers today – and all who come to the Bible, and who come to Jesus, looking for help – can find fresh hope in him. The bishop raised his head from his hands and looked around the room. All the problems were still there, and he was going to have a hard day dealing with them. But he was part of the Story, the Story of the Servant. And the Servant would be with him in all of them, bringing his gentle healing touch wherever it was needed.

MATTHEW 12.22–32

Jesus and Beelzebul

[22]They brought to Jesus a man who was possessed by a demon that made him unable to see or speak. Jesus healed him, so that the sick man was able to talk and see. [23]All the crowds were astonished.

'He can't be David's Son, can he?' they said.

[24]The Pharisees heard this.

144

'The fellow can only cast out demons', they said, 'because he's in league with Beelzebul, the prince of demons!'

25 Jesus knew their thoughts.

'Suppose a kingdom is split down the middle,' he said to them. 'It'll go to rack and ruin! If a city or a household is split down the middle, it's doomed! 26 And if the satan drives out the satan, he's split down the middle – so how can his kingdom stay standing?

27 'What's more, if I cast out demons by Beelzebul, whose power are your people in league with when they cast them out? Yes, they'll tell you what's what! 28 But if I'm casting out demons because I'm in league with God's spirit – well, then, God's kingdom has arrived on your doorstep!

29 'Look at it like this. Suppose you want to break into a strong man's house and steal his belongings. How are you going to do that unless you first tie up the strong man? Then you can plunder his house to your heart's content. 30 If you're not with me, you're against me. Unless you're gathering the flock with me, you're scattering it.

31 'So let me tell you this: people will be forgiven for every sin and blasphemy; but blasphemy against the spirit will not be forgiven. 32 If anyone speaks a word against the son of man, it will be forgiven. But if anyone speaks a word against the holy spirit, it won't be forgiven, either in the present age or in the age to come.'

'How did they do it?'

We stood looking up at the west front of one of France's great medieval cathedrals. It was massive, majestic and awe-inspiring. At the same time, the overall shaping of the stone was so beautifully worked that it seemed to float in the air, as though it might almost be a gateway into **heaven**. A builder in the twenty-first century would find it a daunting task to do anything like it, even with all the modern technology available. How did they do it a thousand years ago?

I don't know the answer to that question, but you hear it

asked of many great achievements. We watch as a young violinist storms through a concerto; we are awed at the combination of the majestic sweep of the music and the apparent effortlessness which leaves the sound floating in the air. How, we ask, does she do it? It's the natural question to ask when we see something that seems way beyond our normal capabilities.

It's the question they asked about Jesus; and ultimately there were only two sorts of answers they could give. The healings he was doing were not the sort of thing you could achieve by brilliant artistry and technology, like the medieval architects and builders. Nor was it a matter of practising for long, hard hours like the musician, so as then to be able to perform on stage with apparent ease. No: there was a power at work, a power that put most other powers to shame. It was coming from somewhere. And Jesus' opponents thought they knew where.

It was the prince of **demons** himself, they said. 'Beelzebul' is a kind of jokey name for the arch-demon or devil, '**the satan**', the accuser. It literally means 'Lord of flies' or 'Lord of filth', though in Jesus' day it was most likely just a kind of slang term, a way of avoiding speaking directly of the devil. But why did they think Jesus might be in league with the arch-demon?

Because the alternative was that he really was acting in the power and **spirit** of Israel's God himself. That would mean that everything else he was doing – welcoming outcasts, announcing the **kingdom** in a way which stood everything upside down, refusing to endorse a programme of national liberation – all this would be God's work, even though it seemed, to the **Pharisees** at least, as though it was going in exactly the opposite direction to what they thought God wanted.

So it wasn't just a very serious accusation, though it was that as well. It was tantamount to a charge of witchcraft. If enough people thought Jesus was dabbling in black arts, that would be the end of him, soon enough. It was a way of rejecting his whole programme, his entire kingdom-movement.

One of the many interesting things about this charge is that it shows, to anyone who might have wondered whether Jesus really was doing all these extraordinary things recorded by Matthew and the others, that, as a matter of sober history, he must have been. Only someone doing the sort of remarkable healings recorded in the **gospels** would incur a charge like this. You don't say, 'How do they do it?' when you're standing beside an ordinary house, or watching an amateur musician struggling through a not-very-difficult piece of music. They would only say, 'How does he do it?' of Jesus if he really was performing extraordinary deeds. And we can be sure that the early church, Jesus' devoted followers after his **resurrection**, would never have made up the idea that people said Jesus himself was in league with the devil. No; something like this must have taken place, and for the reasons Matthew gives.

Jesus' answers to the charge are almost as breathtaking as the healings themselves. He sends the accusations straight back in a series of counter-questions and counter-charges. The idea of the satan undoing his own work is ridiculous, he says. One can imagine the satan giving someone power to levitate, for instance, or to gain wealth or fame, but if he gives him power to undo other aspects of his own, that is, satanic, work he really must be mad. If I am trying to build a house I'm unlikely to call in a contractor and give him authority to demolish parts of it. If the satan is wanting to get more and more control over people he's unlikely to give Jesus power to set lots of them free.

In addition, there are other Jewish exorcists whose work meets with some success at least; are they in league with the devil as well? Of course not. Rather, Jesus' work is a sign of something that his contemporaries were longing for deeply, but were not expecting to look like this. God's kingdom was coming upon them, bursting in as a force, a power to be reckoned with, coming as the only true answer to the question, How is Jesus doing it?

In fact (verses 29–30) what Jesus is doing is a sign of something he's *already* done. If he's now helping himself to the property of 'the strong man', it can only be because he's already tied him up. First you have to win the victory over the satan (our minds, of course, go back to Matthew 4.1–11); then you can plunder his possessions. There is a sobering word there for all who seek to advance God's kingdom. Are we prepared to go the long, hard route of first winning the victory over temptation?

Jesus' final warning has often worried devout readers. How can we know whether or not we have committed this unforgiveable sin? But this saying relates very specifically to what has gone before. Jesus is warning against looking at the work of the spirit and declaring that it must be the devil's doing. If you do that, it's not just that you *won't* be forgiven; you *can't* be, because you have just cut off the very channel along which forgiveness would come. Once you declare that the only remaining bottle of water is poisoned, you condemn yourself to dying of thirst.

Although the warning is therefore not so worrying at one level as some have imagined – if you're worried about committing this sin, it's a good sign that you haven't done so – it remains serious in terms of the decision people reach about Jesus. It is still possible for people to look at him and say 'he must have been mad', or worse. But if Jesus really was bringing God's kingdom into reality, refusing to recognize it means cutting yourself off from its effects, of which forgiveness is one of the chief ones. When we look at Jesus and ask, 'How did he do it?', this isn't just a matter of idle curiosity.

MATTHEW 12.33–42

The Sign of Jonah

³³'You must make up your mind between two possibilities,' Jesus went on. 'Either the tree is good, in which case its fruit is

good; or the tree is bad, in which case its fruit is bad. You can tell the tree by its fruits, after all.

³⁴'You're a family of snakes! How can you say good things when you're bad inside? What the mouth speaks is what fills the heart. ³⁵A good person produces good things from a good storeroom; an evil person produces evil things from an evil storeroom. ³⁶Let me tell you this: on judgment day people will have to own up to every trivial word they say. ³⁷Yes: you will be vindicated by your own words – and you will be condemned by your own words.'

³⁸'Teacher,' responded some of the scribes and Pharisees. 'We would like to see a sign from you.'

³⁹'This wicked and immoral generation is looking for a sign,' replied Jesus. 'But no sign will be given to it – except the sign of Jonah. ⁴⁰Jonah, you see, was in the stomach of the sea-monster for three days and three nights – and in the same way the son of man will be in the heart of the earth for three days and three nights. ⁴¹The men of Nineveh will rise up at the judgment along with this generation and will condemn it. They, after all, repented when they heard Jonah's warnings! And, in case you hadn't noticed, something greater than Jonah is here. ⁴²The Queen of the South will be raised at the judgment with this generation and will condemn it. She, after all, came from the ends of the earth to hear the wisdom of Solomon! And, in case you hadn't noticed, something greater than Solomon is here.'

We all like to play at being amateur detectives. Every year another crop of novels appears, and sometimes plays and movies as well, in which a wicked deed has been performed and nobody can figure out who did it. Some of the greatest names in fiction have created almost equally famous heroes and heroines, with Conan Doyle's Sherlock Holmes the best known of a distinguished list.

The ability of the detective lies mainly in this: to spot the one or two most relevant clues out of the mass of information, mostly irrelevant, which blinds the rest of us. As we read the novels, even if we are experienced students of this sort of writing, we all too easily get caught up in the plot, in the lives of the central characters, in the hundred and one fascinating details, and miss the often quite obvious thing that would have told us the truth all along.

Jesus' opponents ask him for a clue, so that they can know the truth of what's going on; but he refuses to provide one. They've got to figure it all out for themselves – and he knows they're not up to it. They have blinded themselves to the real clues that are all around them, and by the time the plot is finally unveiled it will be too late. There will come a time when a clue, and more than a clue, is provided: the **son of man** will be three days and nights 'in the heart of the earth'. This is an odd way of saying 'he will be buried'; Jesus says it like this because it ties in his future fate with the strange fate of the prophet Jonah.

In other words, Jesus' **resurrection**, after he has been thoroughly dead and buried, will be the clue that even his opponents won't be able to miss. But by then the moment will have passed. They will be judged for their failure to read the clues that were, in fact, in front of their noses all along.

Jesus makes the point more strikingly by looking ahead to the day of judgment, and comparing his own Jewish contemporaries unfavourably with certain pagans of old. First, consider the story of the prophet Jonah himself. After his extraordinary escapade with the sea-monster, he preached to the great city of Nineveh, warning that it was about to be overthrown. The people repented of their wickedness, and the city was saved. Second, the Queen of Sheba came (according to 1 Kings 10.1–10), from far away in southern Arabia to listen to the wisdom of King Solomon, reputedly the wisest king of all antiquity.

The people of Nineveh, and the Queen, were both responding to the revealed message of the God of Israel, in the one case through a prophet, in the other through a king. Matthew's reader already knows that Jesus is a prophet, and has come to suspect that he is also the true king, the **Messiah**. Both of these are strikingly confirmed when Jesus declares that something greater than both Jonah and Solomon is here.

This, then, is what the alert first-century detective should have picked up when looking at Jesus – and what the **scribes** and **Pharisees** were failing to see. This passage joins on very closely to what went before, the controversy about whether Jesus was in league with the devil. They are faced, Jesus says, with a choice (verses 33–34). The tree and its fruit are either good or bad. In other words, what Jesus is doing is either good all through or bad all through; either the work of God from top to bottom, or the work of the devil.

The implication is surely clear. They should be able to understand, from looking at what he was doing, healing of all kinds of diseases, that God was indeed at work in him. But Jesus then turns the point around (verses 35–37). If they can't figure out what he is doing, they could at least take warning about their own behaviour. Their speech – and remember that they had just accused Jesus of black magic – will show what's really in their hearts. Casual words always reveal deep attitudes; Jesus said it long before Sigmund Freud did (in the famous 'Freudian slip', the secret someone is trying to hide pops out of their mouth before they can stop it). As a result, casual words will be used on the day of judgment as a reliable indicator of what really matters, the state of the heart.

Jesus' charge against his opponents, then, is that they are like readers of detective fiction who can't spot the clues because they're too busy with their own agendas. The same question presses on us today, both for ourselves and for those who hear the **message** we preach and live. Can we, can they, see to the heart of what's going on in the life and work of Jesus? And can we see to the heart of what's going on in the church and the world today? On judgment day, will the ancient pagans who listened to Jonah and Solomon have to say that we have missed the big and obvious clues, while they picked up the smaller ones?

MATTHEW 12.43–50

Jesus' True Family

[43]'When the unclean spirit goes out of a person,' Jesus continued, 'it goes wandering through waterless places looking for somewhere to rest, and doesn't find anywhere. [44]Then it says, "I'll go back to my house, the one I left." When it gets there it finds it standing empty, clean and tidy. [45]Then it goes out and collects seven other spirits to join it, spirits worse than itself. They go in and take up residence there. The poor person ends up worse off than they were to start with! And that's what will happen with this wicked generation.'

[46]Suddenly, while he was speaking to the crowds, his mother and his brothers came and stood outside, hoping for a chance to speak to him.

[47]'Look,' someone said to him, 'your mother and your brothers are standing outside wanting to speak to you.'

[48]'Who is my mother?' said Jesus to the person who had spoken to him. 'Who are my brothers?'

[49]Then he stretched out his hand towards his disciples.

'Look!' he said. 'Here are my mother and my brothers. [50]Yes; anyone who does what my heavenly father wants is my brother, and my sister, and my mother.'

One of the saddest moments in my pastoral ministry came some years ago when I was contacted by a man in prison. He was coming towards the end of his sentence, having served some years for serious business fraud. During his time in jail he had thought a lot and read a lot. He had come, so it seemed, to a genuine Christian **faith**. He now wanted to learn Greek so he could study the New Testament, and to take up other parts of theological study. I and others helped him all we could. He seemed genuine, sincere, a good student, humble and eager to learn.

Then, when he was released at the end of his sentence, I started to hear disturbing things. He had forged some refer- ences to try to get a job. He was using false identities. When I confronted him about it, he waved it away; it was all a muddle, he said, caused by someone else, and was sorted out now. I never heard from him again. Alas; the house had been swept, tidied and put in order, but the habit of lying, of creating false worlds and living in them, had returned at once, and the good resolutions of his humiliating jail term had all disappeared.

Of course there are many people who succeed in making a genuine and lasting personal reformation after being punished for criminal activity. It can and does happen. But the story illustrates all too well the point Jesus was making: reformation needs to be long-lasting to be genuine. He wasn't just talking about individuals, but about the whole generation of people, his contemporaries, the people who heard his preaching and saw what he was doing.

In what sense did they need to reform? Well, there had been various attempts over the previous years to bring about revival or renewal in Judaism. Two hundred years before Jesus' day there was a great upheaval after a pagan ruler (Antiochus Epiphanes, the megalomaniac King of Syria) had turned the Jerusalem **Temple** into a pagan shrine. Judas Maccabaeus and his colleagues had beaten the Syrians, cleansed the Temple, and established a new royal house that lasted a hundred years. But it didn't solve the problems. Israel remained sinful and compromised.

At least two groups then tried their own reformations, attempting to get to the heart of the problem. The **Pharisees** began as a pressure group trying to get people to keep the

Torah more thoroughly and completely, with a view to liberating Israel inside and out from every kind of paganism. The **Essenes** were an even more rigorous sect, living by their own strict rules. Then, in the years before Jesus' birth and while he was growing up, Herod and his family were rebuilding the Temple, making it one of the most beautiful buildings anywhere in the world. Many believed that YHWH, Israel's God, had abandoned the Temple long ago; maybe he would now return.

Not so, says Jesus. This generation is like a person who has been exorcized, but the **demon** may return and 'repossess' – with several others. All right, you've had your great revolution, and it worked in its way. You have swept and cleaned as best you can, with new programmes of Torah-teaching and personal piety. The Temple itself is standing there, in working order. *But it's still empty.* The demons will return, and this generation will end up worse off than it was before.

It isn't difficult to work out what Jesus meant by all this. His point was not to describe what normally happens when someone is exorcized. If this is what tends to happen after exorcisms, it would be better not to do them in the first place. He was using the danger of 'repossession' to make a sharp comment, at the end of the long discussion of where he got his power from, about the danger that his countrymen were facing. They had had all kinds of reforms, but unless the 'house' got a new 'inhabitant', the demons they had expelled would return with others as well. Arrogance, violence, hatred, darkness, sometimes masquerading as obedience to God's will – all these things would come in and wreck everything. Jesus had urged them to repent of all this, and to accept his **kingdom**-way, but they hadn't done so. They needed to know that they were inviting disaster.

The section finishes with the strange but telling little scene between Jesus and his family. Mark, in a similar passage, tells us that they were themselves anxious about his sanity (3.21); the implication certainly seems to be that Jesus regards their presence as a distraction, an interruption. But the point here is not so much a negative one about his physical family, as a strong and positive one about his **disciples**. They are doing God's will, he declares, by listening to his kingdom-teaching. They are therefore his true family.

For much of this chapter, Jesus has been assailed and attacked by people who regard him and his work as dangerous, subversive and possibly demonic. But there are some people – and here they are, sitting around him! – who are not threatened by this opposition. They are discovering that when they listen to Jesus they are brought into the presence of God, and into knowing and doing his will, in a whole new way.

That, of course, is the challenge for all of us as we study Jesus today. As we listen to what he says, and watch what he does, are we sitting back and criticizing? Are we wanting to interrupt, to say, 'Hold on a minute! Why are you doing it like that?' Or are we learning that by listening in humility, and then acting in obedience, we are brought into a new relationship with the one whom Jesus called 'father'?

MATTHEW 13.1–9

The Parable of the Sower

[1]That very day Jesus went out of the house and sat down beside the sea. [2]Large crowds gathered around him, so he got into a boat and sat down. The whole crowd was standing on the shore.

[3]He had much to say to them, and he said it all in parables.

'Listen!' he said. 'Once there was a sower who went out to sow. [4]As he sowed, some seed fell beside the path, and the birds came and ate it up. [5]Some seed fell on rocky soil, where it didn't have much earth. It sprang up at once because it didn't

155

have depth of soil. ⁶But when the sun was high it got scorched, and it withered because it didn't have any root. ⁷Other seed fell in among thorns, and the thorns grew up and choked it. ⁸And other seed fell into good soil, and produced a crop, some a hundred times over, some sixty, and some thirty times over. ⁹If you've got ears, then listen!'

We stood on the shore of the Sea of Galilee on a spring morning. The bus was up by the road, and we had walked down, several dozen of us, to where the lake was glistening in the sunshine. It was peaceful and still. The ground slopes up steeply from the lakeshore, curving sharply around a narrow inlet. There are several such inlets along the shore just to the west of Capernaum.

Our guide knew what he was doing. He had already asked a local fisherman to bring a small boat. Leaving us on the shore, he got in the boat, and they pushed off and rowed out to the middle of the inlet. Then he stood up in the boat, and in a clear voice, without needing to shout, he read to us this story, the **parable** of the sower. We were amazed. His voice came to us across the water, clear and crisp in the morning air. The steep banks of the inlet acted like a well-designed theatre with perfect acoustics. We stood there listening, imagining a crowd many times larger than ourselves listening to another voice from another boat 2,000 years before. Jesus had discovered a perfect way to speak to several hundred at once, and to have them all hear what he was saying.

Jesus is not the only one who knew what he was doing. Matthew, in collecting together the parables which form this long chapter, has put them more or less at the centre of his whole **gospel**. Chapter 13 is the third of the five 'discourses' which make up the book (Matthew 5—7, 10, 13, 18 and 23—25). These stories draw together all that has been going on so far in the gospel story, and point ahead to what is still to come.

156

In particular, several of the parables look ahead to the warnings of a great coming judgment, in which God will establish the **kingdom** once and for all by rooting out all wickedness.

But is that what these stories are basically about? Didn't most of Jesus' hearers already believe that there would come a time when God would judge the world, dividing the righteous from the wicked? Didn't they long for that day, when they (the righteous, of course) would be rescued from oppression, and their enemies (the wicked, of course) would be punished severely?

Yes, they did; and they wouldn't have come to stand around a lakeside inlet just to hear somebody saying that. They came for quite a different reason. They came because they were starting to guess that the judgment was already beginning, and that Jesus was part of it. They came because they hoped he would tell them more about the way in which the one true God was beginning his work of rescuing them from their enemies then and there, and wanting them perhaps to help in the process. They had plenty of ideas about that, not least the kind of military revolution that many favoured. Was this new prophet going to issue some kind of a call to arms?

What they wanted was, of course, for the old prophecies to be fulfilled. They heard in the synagogues, and some of them studied for themselves, the sacred writings from long ago which spoke of the long period of God's anger against his rebellious people – and then of a new day dawning. On that new day, they would be rescued from evil. Like a farmer starting a new agricultural year, God would sow his field with crops that would bring in a harvest. Isaiah, Jeremiah and others had spoken in this way. Seedtime and harvest, part of God's created order, had long been a picture of how God the creator would act to redeem his people from their sins, rescue them from **exile**, deliver them from oppression.

And now here was a young prophet, doing remarkable things

which made people wonder if he was the one who would bring it all about. No wonder they followed him. And no wonder, when he began to speak about a farmer sowing seed, they listened eagerly, standing still on the shore, resenting any noise or wind that might mean missing a word, while he sat (in that culture, teachers sat down and pupils stood up) in the boat.

But the story he told wasn't exactly what they were expecting. It wasn't a story about God sowing Israel in its own land at last, restoring its fortunes to the sort of greatness they had always dreamed of. It was a story of both failure and success. It was cryptic. When Jesus said, 'If you've got ears, then hear!' this should alert us to the fact that he meant, 'I know this isn't obvious; you're going to have to think about it!' Jesus wanted them to struggle with what he was saying, to talk about it among themselves, to think it through.

What would they have come up with as they did so? Some, I think, might have thought it was a coded way of telling the story of Israel. God sent kings, prophets, **priests**, and none of them really succeeded; now he was sending someone who would. Just like seed in a field; some going to waste, but at last some bearing fruit. That would be **good news** all right.

Others might have thought it was a very strange story. What sort of a farmer wastes two-thirds of the seed like that? Maybe Jesus was exaggerating the normal problems of farming in rugged hill country to make a point, but what could that point be? Was God having difficulty with his project of establishing the kingdom? Were they going to have to wait even longer? What sort of great harvest did Jesus think was going to happen – a hundredfold yield was quite spectacular! How would that come about?

But nobody would have missed the underlying meaning. Yes, Jesus was saying; what you have been longing for and praying for really is coming true. I'm here to make it happen. It's going to be hard for you to understand, but that doesn't mean it isn't true. Stick with me. Listen to me. Figure it out. Come back for more.

Like the crowds on the lakeshore that day, our task, again and again as we read scripture and think about God's work in our own day, is to think it through and figure it out. Matthew's gospel is designed to help us do that. It won't always be easy. Christianity isn't about cosy little lessons to make us feel better. It's about what God's doing in the world – what he's already done in Jesus and what he wants to do through us today. What sort of stories ought we to be telling to get people to listen? Where can we tell them so that people will be able to hear, like the crowds on the lakeshore?

MATTHEW 13.10–17

The Reason for Parables

[10]His disciples came to him.

'Why are you speaking to them in parables?' they asked.

[11]'You've been given the gift of knowing the secrets of the kingdom of heaven,' he replied, 'but they haven't been given it. [12]Anyone who already has something will be given more, and they will have plenty. But anyone who has nothing – even what they have will be taken away! [13]That's why I speak to them in parables, so that they may look but not see, and hear but not understand or take it in. [14]Isaiah's prophecy is coming true in them:

You will listen and listen but won't understand,
You will look and look but not see.
[15]This people's heart has gone flabby and fat,
Their ears are muffled and dull,
So they won't be able to see with their eyes,
Or hear with their ears, or know in their heart,
And they won't turn again and be healed.

¹⁶But there's great news for *your* eyes: they can see! And for your ears: they can hear! ¹⁷I'm telling you the truth: many prophets and holy people longed to see what you see and didn't see it, and to hear what you hear and didn't hear it.'

We went out one windy day to plant a row of trees. The storms of the previous winter had damaged some of the oaks that surrounded the ancient church, and we had decided to remove them and plant new ones.

The actual planting was to be done by some local school-children, aged between seven and nine. They had never planted trees before. Some of them, I think, had never before wondered how a tree came to be there. We stood beside the small holes already dug for the planting, looking at the trees that were still healthy and strong.

'How long d'you think they've been growing for?' asked the schoolteacher. The children squinted up at the great old trees.

'Fifty years?' said one.

'A hundred years?' said another.

'No,' said the teacher. 'About two hundred years, actually. And they're still growing.'

The children looked at each other in amazement.

'My dad's 42,' said one, thoughtfully.

'My mum's 35,' said another, with the same idea struggling to find expression.

'So how long will it take', said a third, 'before these trees we're planting are grown up?'

The teacher smiled. 'A hundred years at least,' she said. 'Why don't you come back when you're 150 and see how they're doing?'

Like an architect designing a great cathedral, when you plant a tree you do so in the knowledge that you won't live to see it grow to full height.

In this passage, Jesus looks back at the time when people had planted the seeds of the **kingdom of heaven**. Prophets had spoken of it. Holy people had prayed for it to come. Hard-working, faithful people had tilled the ground, studied the scriptures, longed for the kingdom. And they had died before it arrived.

Now, by the lakeshore, Jesus was saying that his **disciples**, young men who hadn't done all that, were seeing the day dawn at last. They were like small children standing beside great oak trees planted hundreds of years before. And, like those children, they only partly understood what was happening and how it would all work out.

They thought, most likely, that to plant the kingdom of heaven you simply had to declare that it was now happening, and to go off and fight whatever battles would be necessary to bring it about. That's what other kingdom-movements looked like in Jesus' day. You'd know it was true when you won the battle, when God gave you the victory.

So why, they wondered, was Jesus telling these stories that people could only partly understand? Why wasn't he rousing the crowds to action? Why was he making them think and not telling them the answers? We can feel their frustration, like a child wanting the tree to be fully grown straight away. 'Why do you speak to them in **parables**?'

Jesus' answer is almost as confusing and disturbing as the parable itself. He takes them back once again to the prophets, to a passage in the book of Isaiah which spoke of the reaction the prophet knew his words would provoke. The Israel of his day was wicked and hard-hearted, and, though his message did indeed contain the promise of salvation, that promise could only come true on the other side of an awesome judgment. The great trees would have to come down before the new shoot could start to grow (Isaiah 10.33—11.3). God would cut the tree down, and prune it further and further, until there was only a stump left; but he would then reveal that there was new life hidden in the stump (Isaiah 6.9–13).

And what was that life? 'The holy seed' (6.13). Jesus quotes the very passage in which the prophet promises that one day, many years hence, a new seed, a new shoot, would arise, bringing mercy the other side of judgment. And he does so in order to explain the reason for telling all these stories about – yes – seeds.

The really troubling thing about this passage is not simply that people have had to wait so long to see the kingdom finally appear. The biggest problem is that, now that it is appearing at last, it is bringing both judgment and mercy. And part of the judgment is that people will look and look and not see what God is doing. People will listen and listen to what Jesus is saying and they simply won't be able to understand. Like tone-deaf people listening to a symphony, they will have no idea what it's all about.

Jesus sees this happening and realizes that even this is not outside the purposes of God. His closest followers will understand, indeed are already beginning to understand, though there is much still to come that they, too, will find hard. They are truly seeing and hearing things that God's people of old longed to see and hear. But the tree must be cut down to its stump. Judgment must fall on God's unfaithful people before mercy can grow up instead. And, hidden within this warning, there is the promise: Jesus will himself go ahead of his people and take the brunt of that judgment on himself.

All this is in the future. The reason the disciples can't understand why Jesus has to teach like this is closely related to the reason they won't understand why he has to go to Jerusalem to die on a cross. The reason for speaking in parables is part of the inner core of meaning of Jesus' whole ministry.

Parables, then, aren't simply nice, friendly illustrations designed to help people get their minds round deep abstract truth. In fact, the truth they speak of isn't abstract at all: it's what God is doing personally, bodily, in Jesus and his work, and what God will do through his death and **resurrection**. God is indeed sowing Israel again, planting his people once more, through Jesus. But it doesn't look like what most people were expecting.

Are we ready for the unexpected? Are we too in danger of deciding so firmly what God ought to be doing in our lives, our churches, our world that we become blind and deaf to him when he tries to tell us that it's actually going to be rather different?

MATTHEW 13.18–23

The Parable of the Sower Explained

[18]'All right, then,' Jesus continued, 'this is what the sower story is all about. [19]When someone hears the word of the kingdom and doesn't understand it, the evil one comes and snatches away what was sown in their heart. This corresponds to what was sown beside the path. [20]What was sown on rocky ground is the person who hears the word and immediately receives it with delight, [21]but doesn't have any root of their own. Someone like that only lasts a short time; as soon as there's any trouble or persecution because of the word, they trip up at once. [22]The one sown among thorns is the one who hears the word, but the world's worries and the seduction of wealth choke the word and it doesn't bear fruit. [23]But the one sown on good soil is the one who hears the word and understands it. Someone like that will bear fruit: one will produce a hundred times over, another sixty, and another thirty times over.

I stood still, puzzled. There was a high hedge to my right, and another one to my left. And now there was a third high hedge straight in front of me. The grass was flattened down in this small space. Clearly lots of other people had been here before me. I was in a maze, a huge formal labyrinth, laid out in the garden of a great country house. And now I was thoroughly lost.

I had thought it would be easy, but of course the people who design mazes know you will think that. They lure you in, encouraging you to make decisions about your direction which will then lead you into a series of dead ends. I was in one now. The others in my party, who had scorned my childish desire to try the maze, would be waiting for me. I gave in and took the map out of my pocket.

I then needed to find two things: first, where I was, and second, how to get to where I needed to be. (I was still determined to visit the centre of the maze, even if I hadn't found the way for myself.) Neither was as easy as it seemed. The map itself was full of passageways, and working out which one I'd got into took some time. But I finally worked out where I was, reached the centre, and then found the way out. If I hadn't, I suppose I'd still be in there and you wouldn't be reading this.

Many of Jesus' **parables** are like mazes, designed to challenge his listeners to work out for themselves how to get to the heart of things. But sometimes the hearers simply got lost, and Jesus then provided a map so they could see where they were. There was, actually, an ancient Jewish tradition of providing this kind of explanation, especially after some dramatic and symbolic vision which the person who had seen it (or the people reading about it) might have difficulty working out.

A good example is in Daniel 7, a chapter Jesus and his followers referred to often – perhaps because it was already a favourite among some Jews of their day. The chapter begins with a vision of monsters coming out of the sea, leading to a courtroom scene in heaven where the main monster is condemned and 'one like a **son of man**', in other words a human figure, is vindicated. Then the explanation is given: the four monsters stand for four kingdoms, and the human figure stands for God's people. That's the kind of maze and map some of Jesus' hearers might be familiar with. And that's the kind of maze and map he provides with the parable of the sower, and now with the interpretation.

The point of the map is, first, to help people see where they are in the maze, and then to help them see how to get where they ought to be. As with most mazes, there are several ways of going wrong, but only one way of going right. Jesus has already seen, in the responses of many people to his announcement of God's **kingdom**, that there are certain common reactions which all lead to dead ends; but he knows that there is one reaction which will lead to the person becoming part of God's new work, a kingdom-person who will be like a seed that produces a great harvest.

Before we look at the different ways of getting stuck in the maze, though, it's important to notice how surprising all this would be to the **disciples** themselves, never mind anyone else. They expected, like many Jews of the time, that when God finally acted to bring the kingdom to birth this would happen in a blaze of glory, in a movement that would sweep through Israel, bringing freedom, justice and peace wherever it went, continuing until the whole world had come under God's righteous rule. The suggestion that, instead, it might come as it were by stealth, not only through the puzzling words of a riddling preacher but through the mixed response of his hearers – this must have seemed very strange.

But this was, and remains, God's way of working. There is a good reason for it. If God were simply to declare, on a particular day or even over the space of a few weeks, that his justice would now operate throughout the world, the human race as a whole would stand condemned. Again and again in Jewish thought we find the belief that God must delay his final action in order to give people time to repent, time, under his gentle prompting, to find their way to the heart of the maze. If he acts too speedily, everybody will be caught in their own cul-de-sacs, and nobody will have made it to the middle.

That's why the **word** is so important as a theme in Jesus' ministry and in the early church. Jesus speaks God's word, the word which announces the kingdom. As Isaiah saw, the word goes out and does its own work in people's hearts and lives. That's what some kinds of words do: they change the way people are, inside. They give them an internal map so that they can now find their way themselves.

But not everyone who heard Jesus' words used them like this. Still, today, not everyone who hears them has the right reaction. The interpretation of the parable is, therefore, both very specific to Jesus' own context and very relevant to Christian preaching in our own day. Some allow the evil one to snatch the words away at once. Most of us have experienced cynical and sneering reactions. Some seem to be enthusiastic, but when the **gospel** starts to make demands on them they quickly show that the word never really went down and became rooted in their hearts. Some really do have a deep-rooted hearing of the word, but then allow other things to take root in their hearts as well; like thorns, the other things choke the delicate plant of the word. These are all ways of getting stuck in the maze, of not finding the way to the centre. As we read the parable today, we should ask ourselves: are we, too, stuck somewhere? Are we in danger of any of these reactions?

But then there is the promise of seed that really does bear fruit. According to this map, the way to that is by hearing *and understanding*. This takes time, and sometimes hard work. A quick glance at the scriptures, an occasional sitting in church or a study group and being entertained by some new idea, is probably not enough. Care and thought needs to be put in to the task of hearing the word of the kingdom until it has taken proper root. Stones may need moving from the soil; thorns may need uprooting. But when hearing brings understanding, we know we're getting close to the goal, to the heart of the maze. And the promise then is this: not just that we will, as it were, have succeeded for our own sake, but that we will in turn become kingdom-people, bearing fruit in our own right.

MATTHEW 13.24–35

The Parable of the Weeds

[24]He put another parable to them.

'The kingdom of heaven', he said, 'is like this! Once upon a time a man sowed good seed in his field. [25]While the workers were asleep, his enemy came and sowed weeds in among the wheat, and went away. [26]When the crop came up and produced corn, then the weeds appeared as well.

[27]'So the farmer's servants came to him.

'"Master," they said, "didn't you sow good seed in your field? Where have the weeds come from?"

[28]'"This is the work of an enemy," he replied.

'"So," the servants said to him, "do you want us to go and pull them up?"

[29]'"No," he replied. "If you do that you'll probably pull up the wheat as well, while you're collecting the weeds. [30]Let them both grow together until the harvest. Then, when it's time for harvest, I will give the reapers this instruction: 'First gather the weeds and tie them up in bundles to burn them, but gather the wheat into my barn.'"'

[31]He put another parable to them.

'The kingdom of heaven', he said, 'is like a grain of mustard seed, which someone took and sowed in a field. [32]It's the smallest of all the seeds, but when it grows it turns into the biggest of the shrubs. It becomes a tree, and the birds in the sky can then come and nest in its branches.'

[33]He told them another parable.

'The kingdom of heaven is like leaven,' he said, 'which a woman took and hid inside three measures of flour, until the whole thing was leavened.'

³⁴Jesus said all these things to the crowds in parables. He didn't speak to them without a parable. ³⁵This was to fulfil what was spoken by the prophet:

I will open my mouth in parables,
I will tell the things that were hidden
Since the very foundation of the world.

'Why doesn't God *do* something?'

That is perhaps the most frequent question that people ask Christian leaders and teachers – and those of some other faiths, too. Tragedies happen. Horrific accidents devastate lives and families. Tyrants and bullies force their own plans on people and crush opposition, and they seem to get away with it. And sensitive souls ask, again and again, why is God apparently silent? Why doesn't he step in and stop it?

These **parables** are not a direct answer to the question, and probably no direct answer can be given in this life. But they show, through the various different stories, that God's sovereign rule over the world isn't quite such a straightforward thing as people sometimes imagine.

Would people really like it if God were to rule the world directly and immediately, so that our every thought and action were weighed, and instantly judged and if necessary punished, in the scales of his absolute holiness? If the price of God stepping in and stopping a campaign of genocide were that he would also have to rebuke and restrain every other evil impulse, including those we all still know and cherish within ourselves, would we be prepared to pay that price? If we ask God to act on special occasions, do we really suppose that he could do that simply when we want him to, and then back off again for the rest of the time?

These parables are all about waiting; and waiting is what we all find difficult. The farmer waits for the harvest-time, watching in frustration as the weeds grow alongside the wheat. Not only the farmer, but also the birds, wait for the tiny mustard seed to grow into a large shrub. The woman baking bread must wait for the leaven to spread its way through the dough until the whole loaf is mysteriously leavened. And that's what God's **kingdom** is like.

Jesus' followers, of course, didn't want to wait. If the kingdom was really present where Jesus was, coming to birth in what he was doing, then they wanted the whole thing at once. They weren't interested in God's timetable. They had one of their own, and expected God to conform to it.

Notice, in particular, what the servants say about the weeds. They want to go straight away into the cornfield and root out the weeds. The farmer restrains them, because life is never that simple. In their zeal to rid the field of weeds they are very likely to pull up some wheat as well.

Did Jesus, perhaps, have an eye here on the revolutionary groups of his day, only too ready to step into God's field and pull up what looked like weeds? There were many groups, including some of the **Pharisees**, who were eager to fight against pagans on the one hand and against compromised Jews on the other. These 'servants' may have intended to do God's will. They were longing for God to act, and were prepared to help him by acting themselves. But part of Jesus' whole campaign is to say that that the true kingdom of God doesn't come like that, because God himself isn't like that.

At the heart of the parable of the weeds and the wheat is the note of patience – not just the patience of the servants who have to wait and watch, but the patience of God himself. God didn't and doesn't enjoy the sight of a cornfield with weeds all over the place. But nor does he relish the thought of declaring harvest-time too soon, and destroying wheat along with weeds.

Many Jews of Jesus' time recognized this, and spoke of

God's compassion, delaying his judgment so that more people could be saved at the end. Jesus, followed by Paul and other early Christian writers, took the same view. Somehow Jesus wanted his followers to live with the tension of believing that the kingdom was indeed arriving in and through his own work, and that this kingdom would come, would fully arrive, not all in a bang but through a process like the slow growth of a plant or the steady leavening of a loaf.

This can sometimes seem like a cop-out today, and no doubt it did in Jesus' day as well. Saying that God is delaying his final judgment can look, outwardly, like saying that God is inactive or uncaring. But when we look at Jesus' own public career it's impossible to say that God didn't care. Here was one who was very active, deeply compassionate, battling with evil and defeating it – and still warning that the final overthrow of the enemy was yet to come.

We who live after Calvary and Easter know that God did indeed act suddenly and dramatically at that moment. When today we long for God to act, to put the world to rights, we must remind ourselves that he has already done so, and that what we are now awaiting is the full outworking of those events. We wait with patience, not like people in a dark room wondering if anyone will ever come with a lighted candle, but like people in early morning who know that the sun has arisen and are now waiting for the full brightness of midday.

MATTHEW 13.36–43

The Parable of the Weeds Explained

³⁶Then Jesus left the crowds and went into the house. His disciples came and joined him.

'Explain to us', they said, 'the parable of the weeds in the field.'

³⁷'The one who sows the good seed', said Jesus, 'is the son of

man. [38]The field is the world; the good seed are the children of the kingdom. The weeds are the children of the evil one; [39]the enemy who sowed them is the devil. The harvest is the close of the age, and the reapers are angels.

[40]'So: when the weeds are gathered and burned in the fire, that's what it will be like at the close of the age. [41]The son of man will send out his angels, and they will collect together out of his kingdom everything that causes offence, and everyone who acts wickedly. [42]They will throw them into the fiery furnace, where there will be weeping and gnashing of teeth. [43]Then the righteous will shine like the sun in the kingdom of their father. If you have ears, then hear!'

I have on my desk a photograph of a sunset. The sun is going down over one of my favourite countryside scenes, lighting up the sky above and silhouetting, on the skyline, hills I have loved since boyhood. The sun is mostly behind a cloud in the photograph; but it is doing its best to break through. If I look hard at it I find it dazzling, even though it's low in the sky, partially clouded, and in any case only a photograph.

Now imagine the sun in the Middle East, on the average day for most of the year. It isn't just dazzling in that sort of way; it's quite terrifying. When it comes up in the morning it can feel truly threatening. People hide from it, finding shady corners, wearing protective hats and veils. When Jesus spoke of people shining like the sun in the **kingdom** of their father, that's the kind of effect he had in mind, not just an attractive glow on the horizon.

So what on earth could he have meant?

C. S. Lewis, in a famous sermon, once declared that every human being, man, woman and child you meet is someone who, if you saw them now as one day they will be, would either make you recoil from them in horror or would strongly tempt you to worship them. It isn't the physical brightness that matters, though it may well be that in God's new world his true children will themselves be sources of light, not merely recipients. What matters is the prestige and status they will have.

This won't have anything to do with privilege or pride. All trace of that kind of thing will have gone for ever. It will have to do with reflecting and embodying the love and glory of God himself; that's what, after all, human beings were meant to do. Each human being was designed to be a God-reflector. That's part of what 'being in God's image' is all about (Genesis 1.26–28). Since we're all different, God intends that each of us should reflect a different facet of his glory. When God's great human harvest is complete, we won't be like hundreds of identical bundles of wheat; we will be as different as the flowers and shrubs in a well-stocked garden, only more so.

Most human languages are inadequate at this point, and have to use pictures. Saying that we will have 'glory' doesn't get us much further. Talk of 'power' is easily misunderstood. But it's clear that what Jesus is talking about is a redeemed, renewed human race that is, at last, what God meant it to be: the mirror in which the rest of creation can see who its creator really is, and can worship and serve him truly. The same mirror in which the world can see the true God will reveal that this God is supremely loving, wise, beautiful, holy, just and true.

When we read the awesome judgment scenes in the Bible, it is that combination of attributes we must learn to see; and this interpretation of the **parable** is one of those scenes. It's all too easy to read about evildoers being thrown into a burning fiery furnace and to conjour up medieval images of hellfire and damnation. It's then all too easy to react against the excesses of some earlier Christian preaching, which tried to frighten people into believing by telling them they'd fry in **hell** if they didn't. We might then deny any doctrine of future judgment at all. Many who have taken this route want to say either that God would never judge or condemn anyone or that he will postpone the harvest until every single weed has been turned into wheat.

There certainly are caricatures of God and his judgment which we should avoid like the plague. God is not a sadistic monster who would happily consign most of his beloved, image-bearing creatures to eternal fire. But there are equal and opposite caricatures we should also beware of. God is not an indulgent grandparent determined to spoil the youngsters rotten by letting them do whatever they like and still giving them sweets at the end of the day. We must refuse the second just as firmly as the first.

Anyone who can't see that there is such a thing as serious and vicious evil in the world, after all that's happened in the twentieth century and is still happening now in the twenty-first, is simply wearing the wrong spectacles. Anyone who doesn't hope and pray that the God who made the world will one day put it to rights is condemning themselves to regarding the world as, at best, a sick joke. But anyone who supposes that the true and living God, the world's creator, can put it to rights without confronting, and defeating, not only 'evil' in the abstract but those who have given their lives and energies to inventing and developing wickedness, profiting from it, luring others into it, and wreaking large-scale human devastation as a result, is asking for the moon.

This is not to say that only large-scale and obvious wickedness will face God's judgment. There are, as we have seen, stern words in the **gospels** about all of us being judged on every idle word we utter. This passage is not the place to discuss the finer points of how God's people become God's people, granted that every single human (except Jesus himself) is sinful. The parable, with its interpretation, isn't that kind of story. It works with the stark categories that Jesus' hearers were familiar with: wheat and weeds, good and bad, righteous and sinners.

But within that deliberately oversimple story line the parable challenged them to the core, and it should do the same to us. It wasn't as obvious as they had thought who were the weeds and who were the wheat. It was up to God to make that judgment; and God was delegating that judgment to this strange figure, 'the **son of man**', the one who had been sowing the good seed, the one who, as Jesus' hearers would realize, stood for Jesus himself.

Much of this passage looks back, once more, to the book of Daniel. 'The son of man' echoes chapter 7, where 'one like a son of man' is given the right to judge and rule over the monsters who have oppressed God's people. The 'fiery furnace' echoes the passage about Daniel's friends in chapter 3. 'The righteous shining like the sun' reminds us of Daniel 12.3, a prediction of the resurrected glory of God's people. Daniel was a favourite book among Jesus' contemporaries, predicting (so they thought) the soon-to-come victory of Israel over the nations.

Jesus was warning them that, though what they were hoping for would indeed come soon, God's judgment might not be as straightforward as they thought. They needed to think it through afresh in the light of Jesus himself and what he was doing. That's why even the interpretation of the parable ends with the command, 'If you have ears, then hear!' And if Jesus' own hearers needed that command, we certainly do as well.

MATTHEW 13.44–53

Other Parables

[44]'The kingdom of heaven', Jesus continued, 'is like treasure hidden in a field. Someone found it and hid it, and in great delight went off and sold everything he possessed, and bought that field.

[45]'Again, the kingdom of heaven is like a trader who was looking for fine pearls, [46]and who found one that was spectacularly

valuable. He went off and sold everything he possessed, and bought it.

⁴⁷'Again, the kingdom of heaven is like a net that was thrown into the sea, and collected every type of fish. ⁴⁸When it was full, the fishermen brought it to shore. They sat down and selected the good ones, which they put into a bucket; but they threw out the bad ones. ⁴⁹That's what it will be like at the close of the age. The angels will go off and separate the wicked from the righteous, ⁵⁰and they will throw them into the fiery furnace, where there will be weeping and gnashing of teeth.'

⁵¹'Have you understood all this?' asked Jesus.

'Yes,' they answered.

⁵²'Well, then,' he said to them, 'every scribe who has been trained for the kingdom of heaven is like a householder who brings out of his storeroom some new things and some old things.'

⁵³When Jesus had finished these parables, he went away from there.

I went last week to the final concert in a great music festival. The hall (a cathedral, actually) was packed to overflowing. It was a fine summer evening, and everyone had come determined to enjoy themselves.

The two main pieces of music that were played were both beautiful, wonderfully performed, and rapturously received. But it's safe to say that if the advertisement had only mentioned the first of them, not many people would have come. The first piece was a little-known concerto by a little-known composer; the second was a well-known and popular symphony by a famous composer. But the festival organizers had done their work well. They knew that the well-known work would bring the crowds in, and that, once they were there, the same people would be delighted to discover the little-known work, a piece of real passion and power.

Jesus' saying about the householder who produces from his

storeroom some new things and some old things is making that sort of point, only sharper. For him, the 'new' things are the extraordinary, brand new visions that the **kingdom of heaven** is bringing. The 'old' things are the wisdom of the centuries, particularly the ancient stories and hopes of Israel. The **gospel** he brings – and the gospel that Matthew is concerned to tell us about – consists in bringing the two together, rooting the new deep within the old, and allowing the old to come to fresh and exciting expression in the new.

Perhaps Matthew is hinting – only he, after all, has this saying about the householder – that this is his own special vision of what a Christian **scribe** should be like. Perhaps, in fact, he means it not least as a description of the book he's writing, in which precisely this combination of old and new is what strikes us again and again. Jesus and his kingdom-message are meant to startle us; but part of the really shocking thing is that, when we blink and rub our eyes, we see that they are the true fulfilment of the long story of God and Israel, and indeed of God and the world. This chapter, with these **parables**, is the central point in Matthew's gospel (note the way in which verse 53 echoes and prepares for the other section-endings: 7.28, 11.1, 19.1 and 26.1). As we saw at the end of chapter 7, the *shape* of the book is meant to look back to the old and familiar pattern, reminding the careful reader of the five books of Moses; but the book's *content* is new and explosive.

If that's so, then there's a decision to be made, and made urgently. The gospel of the kingdom isn't a pleasant religious idea that you might like to explore some time when you've got an hour or two to spare. It isn't like an attractive object in a museum that you might visit and look at admiringly the next time you're in the district. It's like a fabulous hoard of treasure, yours for the taking – if you'll sell everything else to buy the field where it's hidden. It's like the biggest, finest, purest pearl that any jeweller ever imagined, and it's yours for the taking –

if you'll sell everything else, including all the other pearls you've ever owned, in order to purchase it.

The two little parables at the start of this section cut right across the idea, fashionable in the ancient world as well as the modern one, that the different religions, and the experiences they offer, are like a set of pearls which you could collect. There is only one great pearl; there is only one hoard of treasure; and everything else is as nothing beside it. The pearl, the treasure, is the gospel of the kingdom which Jesus was announcing and embodying. That is the shock, the new thing. Without that, all you've got is the old thing, the same old story that half the world believed then and believes still.

The decision is all the more urgent because the world isn't simply going round and round in circles, as many religions and philosophies teach. It's going in a straight line towards a goal, and it's going there quite fast. The coming of Jesus began the process of final judgment. As he taught and lived the kingdom, the world was divided sharply into two, into those who were swept off their feet by him and those who resisted and rejected his gospel.

That process continued through the first generation. It reached a climax when the city and regime that had rejected Jesus was destroyed by the Romans in AD 70. It continues still, and will do so until the day when God will remake the whole world in justice and truth, and all who have shaped and formed themselves around injustice and lies will find that they are like the bad fish that the fishermen will be forced to throw away. The choice is real, stark and sharp.

The parables in this chapter are a challenge to us at two levels: understanding and action. Understanding without action is sterile; action without understanding is exhausting and useless. As we ponder Jesus' stories and think about what they meant then and mean now, we should always be asking ourselves: what might it mean *today* to be 'a scribe trained for the kingdom of heaven'? How can we be sure, in our thinking, our speaking and our living, that we are both rooted in the old and also bearing the new, fresh fruit of the kingdom of heaven?

MATTHEW 13.54–58

Opposition in Nazareth

[54]Jesus came to the town where he had been brought up. He taught them in their synagogue, and they were astonished.

'Where did this fellow get this wisdom, and these powers?' they said.

[55]'Isn't he the carpenter's son? Isn't his mother called Mary, and his brothers James, Joseph, Simon and Judah? [56]And aren't all his sisters here with us? So where does he get it all from?' [57]They were offended by him.

So Jesus said to them, 'No prophet lacks respect – except in his own town and his own house!'

[58]And he didn't perform many mighty works there, because they didn't believe.

She came home from school with all the wide-eyed excitement of an eager eight-year-old, clutching the clarinet case to her like a favourite teddy bear. She had had her first music lesson on the new instrument that morning. She couldn't wait to get the instrument out and show it to her parents.

She put the music carefully on the shiny new stand. She adjusted the reed the way she'd been shown. Suddenly conscious of her audience, she tried to play the little tune the teacher had taught her. As with every other beginner, some of the notes sounded right, but several came out with a squawk like a distressed hen.

Her father, tired after a long working day, couldn't bear it. Her mother, trying to say the right thing, suggested she go and play the tune in the other room. She held back her tears until she was out of the door. A few squawks could be heard from the other room, then silence. Within a few weeks the clarinet had been returned to the school and the lessons cancelled. Ten years later, when I met her, the memory of rejection was still fresh and unhealed.

All right, we think; we know that families are often less tolerant of their own members than of people from outside. We know that people are often ready to learn new things from other people but not from their parents or children. But surely, we think, Jesus should have been different? After all, he was . . . well, he was Jesus, the **son of God**, the greatest teacher the world had ever known! Surely his own family and village would welcome him with open arms?

Part of the whole point of the **gospel** is that Jesus wasn't an exception. He was, and is, one of us. As John says, he came to his own and his own didn't receive him. He's the boy from down the street, they said. He's just a local lad – and here are his brothers and sisters still living with us. He can't be anyone special. Perhaps it requires a particular kind of humility to hear something new and disturbing from someone very familiar. Certainly it required something the people of Nazareth didn't have.

Matthew places this incident right after the long series of Jesus' **parables** of the **kingdom**, and it's a stark warning to anyone who might suppose that Jesus' teaching was meant to be a matter of simple and straightforward lessons about life, morality, spirituality or whatever, that anyone with half a brain would pick up easily. Far from it. This 'teaching', if we want to call it that, is shocking, explosive and dangerous. Sensible people would be worried about it. People who had known the 'teacher' from boyhood would be tempted to doubt whether he could possibly be serious. Perhaps he should go and play this funny tune out in the back yard. Better still, in the next town.

Jesus' rejection at Nazareth foreshadows, of course, the wider rejection of his message and ministry by his Jewish contemporaries as a whole. Their challenge to his prophetic and healing powers is a distant sign of the violent challenge that would come from the chief **priests**, and the Roman soldiers, right at the end. And it reminds us (though people with experience of Christian ministry will scarcely need too much reminder) that preaching the gospel is never easy, never something that can be done, as it were, on auto-pilot. If it is truly Jesus we're talking about, it's the Jesus whose own townsfolk didn't want to believe in him.

At the same time, there is comfort and encouragement hidden in this story too, if we know where to dig for it. The very people the villagers refer to – Jesus' mother, Mary, and his brothers, James, Joseph, Simon and Judah – seem at this point to have joined in the general disapproval. But all that changed. After Jesus' **resurrection**, many of his relatives became great leaders in the early church, and none greater than his brother James. Those who at present seem to be hardened against the message can still be reached by a further act of God's love and power.

There is comfort, too, though of a dangerous variety, in Jesus' own comment about the normal fate of prophets. Of course, just because people are offended by what you say, that doesn't mean you are telling the truth, that you are a heaven-sent true prophet. It may simply mean that you're talking a lot of nonsense. But equally, if the signs that God is at work are there elsewhere – as they were abundantly, of course, in Jesus' case – then the fact of rejection, not least in one's own home district, should never be taken as an indication that one is off track, that God has withdrawn his blessing.

In fact, rejection can sometimes be a strange encouragement. Provided we understand such a moment with humility, it can become a further indication, albeit a dark and negative one, that

God is truly at work. If new creation and new life are going forward, those who have invested heavily in the old creation, the old ways of life, are bound to be offended. But make sure, before you use this argument in your own favour, that the offence in question is the gospel itself, and not something about the messenger.

MATTHEW 14.1–12

The Death of John the Baptist

¹At that time Herod the Tetrarch heard reports about Jesus.

²'This fellow must be John the Baptist,' he said to his servants. 'He's been raised from the dead! That's why these powers are at work in him.'

³This is what had happened. Herod had seized John, tied him up and put him in prison because of Herodias, the wife of his brother Philip. ⁴John had been telling him that it wasn't right for him to have her. ⁵Herod wanted to kill him, but he was afraid of the crowd, because they reckoned that John was a prophet.

⁶When Herod's birthday came round, the daughter of Herodias danced for the assembled company, and delighted Herod. ⁷So he swore a great oath that he would give her whatever she requested. ⁸Prompted by her mother, she said, 'Give me – here, on a platter – the head of John the Baptizer!' ⁹The king was sorry; but because of his oaths, and his guests, he gave orders for it to be given to her. ¹⁰He sent to the prison and had John beheaded. ¹¹His head was brought on a platter and given to the girl, and she passed it on to her mother. ¹²His disciples came and took away the body and buried it. Then they came and told Jesus.

Imagine a movie set in a desert. The plot requires that the hero should travel across barren, dusty country for several days, somehow surviving not only the heat and drought but also the attacks of predators.

At the very beginning of the journey, we see a shadow crossing the ground in front of him. We look up and see a huge bird of prey, swooping down as though to attack him. He escapes, but from time to time, as the journey goes on, we see the shadow again and know that danger is not far away.

The traveller is not the only one making the journey. Ahead of him is a friend who has gone on to try to find the way. Suddenly, in the middle of the journey, we see the shadow again, getting bigger and bigger; the predator is coming in for the attack. But the object of the attack is the friend who's gone on ahead. He has ventured too deep into the bird's territory, and pays the ultimate price. As the awful scene recedes, we return to the hero, knowing now only too well what may lie ahead for him as well.

The shadow that falls across Matthew's **gospel** here is the house of Herod: brooding, malevolent, ready to swoop and kill anything that tries to cross its path. Herod the Great tried to kill Jesus as a baby, and failed (2.13–18). Now Herod the Tetrarch – Antipas, one of the many sons of the earlier Herod – is swooping down to attack, halfway through the story. Where, we wonder, is it all going?

John has cleared the path for Jesus, by warning people of the coming **kingdom** and preparing them for the coming king. He has made it clear, in his preaching, that Herod can't be the true king of the Jews, the **Messiah**. His moral life is such a mess that the idea is unthinkable. That's probably what lies behind John's attack on Herod's bizarre marriage, stealing his own brother's wife. It isn't just that Herod is an adulterer, but that such behaviour demonstrates that he can't be the Lord's anointed. But John, in the end, is powerless before the present king. The bird of prey swoops down and destroys him. And we, Matthew's readers, have a clearer idea of what may yet lie in store for the man who is following in John's footsteps.

We also get a clearer idea of what that fate, when it comes, might mean. John dies, you might say, because of Herod's wickedness. Herod has a lust for power; John stands in his way. He has a lust for women; he's already stolen his brother's wife, and now he is aroused by her daughter, his niece. They can twist him round their fingers, not that he took much twisting. He is proud, and drunk, and the two together make him promise more than he intends and deliver more than he should. Herod's failings come together in a rush, and John's death is the result. The prophet who has warned the king and the people of what will happen to the wicked suffers their fate himself. Matthew has put down a marker, a signpost, halfway through his gospel: if this happened to the prophet who went on ahead, this is what will happen to the one who follows.

So he invites us to reflect, as we see the story unfold, on what is taking Jesus himself to his fate, and how we should view it when it comes. Jesus, like John, has urged people to repent. He, like John, has challenged the present powers, though he has done so more cryptically, in riddles that will only become plain and blunt when he arrives in Jerusalem. He has already had the threat of death suspended over him, not just at his birth but when the **Pharisees**, rightly seeing his plans as cutting clean across their own, decide they should get rid of him. And, behind it all, we learn to recognize what every first-century Jew knew well: that anyone announcing the kingdom of God was challenging a power that stood behind even Herod, the power of Caesar himself. Behind the vulture, higher in the sky but watching and waiting, soars the eagle.

Yet even old Herod glimpses a flash of the truth, though he gets it muddled. Jesus, he thinks, is a resurrected John, and that's why he can do these remarkable deeds. We know that's not true; yet we find here just a little hint of what is to come. The remarkable deeds do point to the **resurrection**, but they do so because they are a foretaste of it, not a result. And the resurrection won't turn John into Jesus, or Jesus into anyone else. It will give Jesus himself a life, and a kingdom, beyond the power of Herod or of Caesar himself. It will give him, in fact, all authority in **heaven** and on earth (28.18).

The meaning of Jesus' life is therefore thrown into sharp focus by this sorry little story about Herod, John and a dancing girl. It invites us not only to read on more thoughtfully, but also to examine the story of our own lives, and that of the church today. Where are we called to stand out against wickedness? What threats will we meet if we do? Or – since we can none of us assume that we should identify only with John in this story – what small weaknesses in our lives are we allowing to grow unchecked that might one day produce real wickedness? What Herod-like characteristics are lurking inside us, waiting for a chance to destroy us or others? If we can answer that question honestly, we shall understand all the more why it was necessary that Jesus should go all the way across his lonely desert and, in the end, take the full weight of human wickedness upon himself.

MATTHEW 14.13–22

The Feeding of the Five Thousand

[13]When Jesus heard it, he went away from there in a boat to a deserted spot by himself. The crowds heard it, and followed him on foot from the towns. [14]When he came out and saw the large crowd, he was sorry for them. He healed their sick.

[15]When it was evening, the disciples came to him.

'This is a deserted spot,' they said, 'and it's already getting late. Send the crowds away so that they can go into the villages and buy food for themselves.'

[16]'They don't need to go away,' said Jesus. 'You give them something to eat.'

[17]'All we have here', they said, 'is five loaves of bread and two fish.'

[18]'Bring them here to me,' he said.

¹⁹He told the crowds to sit down on the grass. Then he took the five loaves and the two fish and looked up to heaven. He blessed the loaves, broke them, and gave them to the disciples, and the disciples gave them to the crowds. ²⁰Everybody ate and was satisfied, and they picked up twelve baskets full of broken pieces. ²¹There were about five thousand men who had eaten, besides women and children.

²²Jesus at once made the disciples get into the boat and go on ahead of him to the opposite shore, while he dismissed the crowds.

Come and be a character in this story. There's plenty of room, and there's a lot to learn.

To begin with, cast your mind back to the last time you were really, really sad. After the death of a parent, perhaps, or a close friend. After you didn't get the job you'd set your heart on. After you had to move out of the house you had loved. What you needed and wanted most was to hide away and be quiet. To reflect, perhaps to pray; but above all to be still, and not have people bother you.

Then supposing the quiet place you chose was invaded by hundreds of others. The little church you thought you'd slip inside was full of a wedding party. The lonely hillside where, surely, you could be private was covered in cheerful hikers. How would you react?

Jesus' reaction here is the more remarkable. He had lost **John**, his cousin and colleague. He had lost him in a manner which must have warned Jesus of what lay ahead for him, too. Yet when he slips away to be quiet and alone, the crowds discover and throng all around him. And his reaction is not anger or frustration, but compassion. He translates his sorrow over John, and perhaps his sorrow over himself, into sorrow for them. Before the outward and visible works of power, healing the sick, comes the inward and invisible work of power, in which Jesus transforms his own feelings into love for those in need.

You have come into the story of Jesus, perhaps, because you've been touched yourself by that compassion. Imagine yourself as one of the **disciples** – not a leader, just one of the Twelve, or perhaps one of their other friends or cousins, hanging around on the edge. You see how Jesus cares for people, and you'd like to care for them too. So you think what might be best for them, and come to him with a suggestion. Wouldn't it be good to send them away now, so that they could go and buy food rather than all getting hungry here, miles away from anywhere?

Jesus is always delighted when people around him come up with ideas which show that they're thinking of the needs of others. But often what he has to do is to take those ideas and do something startling with them. If you really care for them, he says, why don't *you* give them something to eat? This is, perhaps, the typical note of vocation. Our small idea of how to care for people gets bounced back at us with what seems a huge and impossible proposal. You protest. I can't do it! I haven't got the time. I haven't got the energy. I haven't got the ability. All I have is . . .

Ah, but that's the next step, and again typical of how God's calling works. By hanging around Jesus, you've had an idea. It wasn't quite in focus, but your main intention – in this case, that the people should be fed – is on target. Jesus proposes achieving that aim by a different means. You say it's impossible – *but you're prepared to give him the little you've got, if it'll be any good*. Of course it means you'll go hungry yourself . . . but by now you're in too deep to stop. Once the power of Jesus' compassion has begun to catch you up in its flow, you can't stop.

What precisely Jesus does with what we give him is so mysterious and powerful that it's hard to describe in words. Imagine yourself standing there, while Jesus, surrounded by thousands of people, takes this pitifully small amount of food, hardly enough for two people, let alone a crowd, and prays over it. He thanks God for it. He breaks it, and gives it to you and the others, and you give it to . . . one person after another after another, without knowing what's happening or how.

Think through how it's happened. Being close to Jesus has turned into the thought of service; Jesus takes the thought, turns it inside out (making it more costly, of course), and gives it back to you as a challenge. In puzzled response to the challenge, you offer what you've got, knowing it's quite inadequate (but again costly); and the same thing happens. He takes it, blesses it, and breaks it (there's the cost, yet again), and gives it to you – and your job now is to give it to everybody else.

This is how it works whenever someone is close enough to Jesus to catch a glimpse of what he's doing and how they could help. We blunder in with our ideas. We offer, uncomprehending, what little we have. Jesus takes ideas, loaves and fishes, money, a sense of humour, time, energy, talents, love, artistic gifts, skill with words, quickness of eye or fingers, whatever we have to offer. He holds them before his father with prayer and blessing. Then, breaking them so they are ready for use, he gives them back to us to give to those who need them.

And now they are both ours and not ours. They are both what we had in mind and not what we had in mind. Something greater and different, more powerful and mysterious, yet also our own. It is part of genuine Christian service, at whatever level, that we look on in amazement to see what God has done with the bits and pieces we dug out of our meagre resources to offer to him.

Within Matthew's story, of course, there is much more going on than simply a remarkable example of Christian vocation. The twelve baskets left over may point to Jesus' intention to restore God's people, the twelve tribes of Israel. Jesus feeding people in the wilderness fits so well with Matthew's theme of Jesus as the new Moses (God gave the Israelites manna, special bread from **heaven**, when they were in the desert in the time of Moses) that we can be sure that Matthew intended us to see this too.

This probably explains why Jesus sent the crowds away as soon as the feeding was over. He didn't want them hanging around and celebrating his power. The likeness with Moses stops there. Jesus was not intending to march through the land at the head of a great crowd, or to win military victories against God's enemies. He was going to achieve at last the loneliness he sought at the start of this passage, hanging desolate on a cross. If you sense a call to follow him, to share his compassion, to give him what you have so that it can be used in his service, you must remember that it cost him everything as well.

MATTHEW 14.23–36

Jesus Walks on Water

23After he had sent the crowds away, Jesus went up the mountain by himself to pray. When evening came he was there by himself. 24The boat had already gone some distance from the shore and was being smashed around by the waves, since the wind was against it.

25At the very dead of night he came towards them, walking on the water. 26The disciples saw him walking on the sea and panicked, thinking it was a ghost. They screamed with terror. 27But Jesus at once spoke to them.

'Cheer up,' he said, 'it's me! Don't be frightened!'

28'If it's really you, Master,' said Peter in reply, 'give me the word to come to you on the water.'

29'Come along, then,' said Jesus.

Peter got out of the boat and walked on the water and came towards Jesus. 30But when he saw the strong wind he was afraid, and began to sink.

'Master,' he yelled, 'rescue me!'

³¹Jesus at once reached out his hand and caught him.

'A fine lot of faith you've got!' he said. 'Why did you doubt?'

³²They got into the boat, and the wind died down. ³³The people in the boat worshipped him.

'You really are God's son!' they said.

³⁴So they crossed over to the land called Gennesaret. ³⁵The men of that region recognized him and sent word to all the surrounding district. They brought all their sick people to him, ³⁶and begged him to be allowed simply to touch the hem of his clothes. And everyone who touched it was cured.

Curiously, only one great picture of this scene has ever been painted (by Conrad Witz in 1444). You might have thought it would make an ideal subject: Jesus as a shimmering figure on the water, the frightened **disciples** huddling in the boat, and Peter, caught between glory and terror, walking on the water towards Jesus and then . . . starting to sink. Perhaps devout artists avoided it because it seemed to show up the great apostle in a bad light. Personally, I find it all the more encouraging. It rings very true to the Christian experience I know, my own and that of many others.

If the previous story (the feeding of the five thousand) can be read as a picture of Christian vocation, this story can be read as a picture of the life of **faith** – or rather, the life of half-faith, faith mixed with fear and doubt, which is the typical state of so many Christians, as it was with the disciples. Matthew isn't too worried about Peter's reputation. It seems to see-saw to and fro, not least (as we shall see) in chapter 16, and then in the final days of Jesus' life. Peter is something of a larger-than-life character anyway: impetuous, ready for anything, tending to act first and think afterwards. An endearing but risky characteristic. Would you rather have a friend who did what seemed the right thing and then worried about it later, or one who spent so much time thinking it all through that it would take weeks to get anything done?

But before we think how the story works for us as individuals, let's think of it first as a picture of our world. We are like the disciples in the boat. They had seen so much of Jesus' power. They had heard his teaching and prayed his prayer. But now they were stuck. Professional fishermen, they were struggling with the oars, unable to make headway against the wind. We too in our world have discovered so much, learned so much, invented so much, and yet are still without power to do many of the things that really matter. We have invented wonderful machines for making war, but nobody yet has found one that will make peace. We can put a man on the moon, but we can't put food into hungry stomachs. We can listen to the songs the whales sing on the ocean floor, but we can't hear the crying of human souls in the next street.

And there, shimmering on the water, is a strange figure, walking towards us. Much of our world knows at least a little about Jesus; but he seems a ghostly image, a mirage or fantasy, unrelated to us and our problems. Some find him frightening. Others wish he'd go away and leave us alone. Even those who believe in him, as the disciples already did, don't know what to expect from him. But he seems to be doing the impossible, and sometimes people get the idea that it would be good to copy him, if only we could. Some people set off with the aim of doing just that: to bring his love and power, his peace and hope, to the needy world.

But then they let their eyes drop for a moment to the waves. Think of surfers on a Californian beach, when suddenly a double-sized wave rears up and threatens them. Now take away the surf-board, the sunshine, the sand on the shore, and replace them with darkness, fear and a howling gale. One man alone against the elements. That's what it often feels like when you try to bring God's love and healing power into the wild night of the world. That's when we need to hear, once more, Jesus' words – a combination, as so often, of rebuke and encouragement: 'Is that really how much faith you have? Why all this doubt?' The moment when we are most strongly tempted to give up is probably the moment when help is, if only we knew it, just a step away.

That's what it's like for each of us in Christian discipleship, again and again. As far as we know, walking on water in the literal sense wasn't something the early Christians expected to do themselves. Paul, facing another shipwreck, never imagined that getting out of the boat and strolling off to the shore was a viable option. So it's likely that Matthew expects his readers to 'hear' this story in terms of their own journey of faith – and their own struggles with doubt.

There are many times when Jesus asks us to do what seems impossible. How can we even begin to do the task he's called us to? How can we even think of doing without that sin which we're asked to give up? How can we really suppose we might be able to develop a serious habit of prayer when we're so frantic and disorganized?

Of course, if like Peter we look at the waves being lashed by the wind, we will conclude that it is indeed impossible. What we are called to do – it's so basic and obvious, but so hard to do in practice – is to keep our eyes fixed on Jesus, and our ears open for his encouragement (even if it does contain some rebuke as well). And our wills and hearts must be ready to do what he says, even if it seems crazy at the time.

MATTHEW 15.1–9

Discussions of Clean and Unclean

¹At that time some Pharisees and scribes came from Jerusalem to Jesus. They had a question for him.

²'Why', they said, 'do your disciples go against the tradition of the elders? They don't wash their hands when they eat their food!'

³'Why', Jesus replied, 'do *you* go against the command of God because of your tradition? ⁴What God said was "Honour your father and mother" and "If anyone speaks evil of father or mother, they must certainly die." ⁵But you say, "If anyone says to father or mother, 'What you might have gained from me is given to God', ⁶they need do no further honour to their father." As a result, you make God's word null and void through your tradition.

⁷'You play-actors! Isaiah had the right words for you in his prophecy:

⁸This people gives me honour with their lips,
Their heart, however, holds me at arm's length.
⁹The worship which they offer me is vain,
Because they teach, as law, mere human precepts.'

All churches have jokes about the power of tradition. How many Anglicans (or Methodists, or Baptists, or Roman Catholics . . . or whatever you like) does it take to change a light bulb? Five, comes the answer: one to change the bulb, and four to talk about how good the old bulb was.

The story is told of an archbishop visiting a local church and meeting a man who had been going there for 50 years. 'You must have seen many changes in that time,' said the archbishop. 'Yes,' replied the man, 'and I opposed them all.' The danger of this approach is highlighted by what some have seen as 'the seven last words of the church', parallel to the 'seven last words' of Jesus on the cross. The 'seven last words', it is suggested, might be these: 'We never did it this way before.'

It is some comfort, perhaps, to know that the problem of tradition and truth has been with the church from its very beginning. And of course the problem is deeper than simply supporting tradition against innovation or innovation against tradition. Novelty for the sake of novelty is just as sterile as custom for the sake of custom. Just as some people like to do things in church the same way year after year, not least when everything else in society is changing so rapidly, so some people like to do things as differently as they can as often as they can. Such personal preferences make a poor basis for wise judgment and decisions.

In any case, the issue at stake between Jesus and the **Pharisees** was not just that he and his followers were doing things a new way instead of the traditional way. That's how the Pharisees wanted to line things up, but Jesus' sharp response shows that it wasn't that easy. They were accusing him of letting his **disciples** go soft on one of the traditional purity codes: handwashing before meals.

This may seem a trivial and unimportant thing to grumble about. Indeed, some people have questioned whether legal teachers would make the journey from Jerusalem to Galilee, as Matthew says in the first verse, just to accuse Jesus and his followers of such a thing. But this misses the point. Jesus was at the head of a movement that was already seen as dangerous. He was doing and saying new things, and crowds of people were flocking to him. In those circumstances, people would look for the little tell-tale signs of whether he was really 'sound' or not, whether he was really in line with 'the way things should be done', or was being disloyal to it. The story makes sense with what we know of other Pharisees. The arch-Pharisee Saul of Tarsus, after all, was on his way from Jerusalem to Damascus, twice as far away, to attack followers of Jesus, when he met the risen Jesus and had his heart and life turned inside out.

Jesus doesn't answer the accusation, though in the next part of the chapter he says things which undermine its force. Here he launches a counter-attack. The Pharisees' traditions have had the effect, he says, of overturning something far more important than tradition, namely scripture itself. The Pharisees, of course, claimed that their traditions were embodying the practical outworking of what scripture taught. Jesus was pointing out that in one particular case the opposite was true.

In the Ten Commandments themselves, the Israelites were commanded to honour their parents. This meant, not least, looking after them in their old age. But in the Pharisees' traditions it was permitted that someone might make a gift to the **Temple** of an equivalent amount to what they might have spent on their parents. If they did that, they were deemed to be under no further obligation. This had an obvious benefit to the Temple, and indeed might give the appearance of great piety. But it undermined the whole point of the **law**.

From this one little example Jesus launches his major attack on the Pharisees: they are play-actors. The word 'hypocrite' literally means someone who puts on a mask to play a part. The mask, says Jesus, is the words the Pharisees use. Behind their words of piety, their hearts have no intention of really discovering what God desired. They have elevated merely human customs to the status of divine commands. In the process, they have overthrown the actual divine commands themselves.

Just as all churches develop jokes about the power of tradition, so all churches, and Christian leaders especially, need to ask on a regular basis whether what they teach, and what they assume Christian people will do, really grow out of scripture itself, or whether they are simply human traditions that may need to be challenged. It isn't simply that something is 'old-fashioned' or 'up to date'. Jesus wasn't just saying 'tradition is dangerous – if in doubt, go for innovation!' In fact, his own criticism of the Pharisees was that their more recent traditions had undermined the ancient and foundational **word** of God. That is why serious study of scripture remains at the heart of the church's life and task, not least for leaders. Unless we are constantly being refreshed and challenged by scripture, we won't have our wits about us to distinguish between healthy and hypocritical traditions – or, for that matter, between life-giving innovations and deadly ones.

MATTHEW 15.10–20

The Parable of Clean and Unclean

[10]Then Jesus called the crowd, and said to them,

'Listen and understand. [11]What makes someone unclean isn't what goes into the mouth. It's what comes out of the mouth that makes someone unclean.'

[12]Then the disciples came to Jesus.

'Do you know', they said, 'that the Pharisees were horrified when they heard what you said?'

[13]'Every plant that my heavenly father hasn't planted', replied Jesus, 'will be plucked up by the roots. [14]Let them be. They are blind guides. But if one blind person guides another, both of them will fall into a pit.'

[15]Peter spoke up. 'Explain the riddle to us,' he said.

[16]'Are you still slow on the uptake as well?' replied Jesus. [17]'Don't you understand that whatever goes into the mouth travels on into the stomach and goes out into the drain? [18]But what comes out of the mouth begins in the heart, and that's what makes someone unclean. [19]Out of the heart, you see, come evil plots, murder, adultery, fornication, theft, false witness, and blasphemy. [20]These are the things that make someone unclean. But eating with unwashed hands doesn't make a person unclean.'

One of the best-loved characters in children's stories is Winnie-the-Pooh. In one escapade of this down-to-earth, loveable toy bear (the creation of the writer A. A. Milne), Pooh attempts to trap an Elephant – or, as he mispronounces it, a Heffalump.

Pooh digs a hole to catch the Heffalump, and decides to bait the trap with some of his own favourite food: honey. But, fond as he is of honey, he can't bear to leave a whole jar of it in the trap, and so begins to eat some himself . . . excusing himself with the thought that it's important to make sure it really *is* honey, all the way down. It wouldn't do to have anything else, perhaps cheese or something, at the bottom. And of course, by the time he's quite sure it really *was* honey all the way down, the jar is empty...

For Pooh what matters is what the jar really contains, all the way down. If it's only got honey at the top, but something quite different underneath, one needs to know. And that lies at the heart of what Jesus now says, by way of comment on the earlier discussion with the **Pharisees** about the purity laws.

What's the point of keeping all the purity laws? In order to be the sort of person God always had in mind. What sort of person did God always have in mind? One who was pure, not just on the surface, but right the way down, down to the very depths of the personality. There wasn't anything wrong with the purity laws themselves, though some of the developed traditions about them may have been fairly pointless. But to stick just with the outward laws, and ignore the call to be pure through and through, was to miss the point entirely.

Jesus' way of putting this was a riddle that must have seemed puzzling and, as this passage says, shocking to his hearers. 'It isn't what goes into the mouth, but what comes out of the mouth, that makes you unclean.' What can he mean? He surely can't be thinking of vomit, or spittle?

He is thinking of words. His point is that words reveal what the person contains, deep down. As we have seen already, long before psychologists noticed that what people say is an indication of what's really going on inside their thoughts and imaginations, particularly when they're not concentrating very hard, Jesus had made the same point. The actions which make someone unclean, unfit for God's holy presence, are things like murder, adultery, fornication and the rest. The motivations which point towards such actions give themselves away in thoughts and words which come bubbling up from the depths of the personality, showing that, whatever outward purity codes the person may keep, the innermost self of that person needs to be changed if they are to be what God intended and wanted.

So this discussion isn't simply about whether Jesus and his followers keep the traditions that the Pharisees maintained and tried to urge on other Jews. The discussion is about what God really wants his people to be like, and how this desire can be fulfilled. Here and elsewhere Jesus is addressing the deep question – which to be sure many of his contemporaries, including many of the Pharisees themselves, were well aware of: how can the human heart be made pure?

Anyone who doesn't see this as a problem – including anyone who supposes that the answer can lie simply in a list of regulations – has not yet seen the depth of wickedness that lurks inside the personality. Most of us are quite capable of most of the things listed in verse 19, and many others besides. If that's what's in our hearts, we are impure in God's eyes, and need to be made clean, clean all the way down.

The point of what Jesus is saying, then, is that through his work God is offering a cure for this deep-level impurity. And this cure cuts across what other teachers of his day were offering. They saw the purity laws as the right place to start, and some of them were content to stop there too. Jesus saw these laws as largely irrelevant to the real task he had come to undertake. He was (as he said in several of the **parables** in chapter 13) sowing the seeds of the **kingdom**, planting plants that would grow and flourish. But people with other agendas were planting plants that would be torn up. People who were pushing the purity laws as the solution to the problems of Israel were, he said, like one blind person trying to show another blind person the way to go. Not only would both of them get lost, but both of them might well fall into a hole in the ground.

The real challenge of this passage, then, comes to all of us, especially if we think of ourselves as followers of Jesus. We may not observe the purity codes of ancient Israel, but are our hearts, our thoughts and intentions, and the casual words we utter, telling us that our own purity is less than complete? If so, what are we doing about it?

Jesus does not, in this passage, offer the remedy for the condition he has diagnosed. That will come through the developing story. Ultimately, he is himself the remedy, as in his death and **resurrection**, and the gift of the **spirit**, he deals with the wickedness and uncleanness that infects the human race. But the remedy needs to be applied to the disease, down and down inside the human personality, so that when we stand before God he will see us, as he always intended, pure through and through, right down to the bottom.

MATTHEW 15.21–28

The Canaanite Woman

²¹Jesus left that place and went off to the district of Tyre and Sidon. ²²A Canaanite woman from those parts came out and shouted, 'Have pity on me, son of David! My daughter is demon-possessed! She's in a bad way!' ²³Jesus, however, said nothing at all to her.

His disciples came up.

'Please send her away!' they asked. 'She's shouting after us.'

²⁴'I was only sent', replied Jesus, 'to the lost sheep of the house of Israel.'

²⁵The woman, however, came and threw herself down at his feet.

'Master,' she said, 'please help me!'

²⁶'It isn't right', replied Jesus, 'to take the children's bread and throw it to the dogs.'

²⁷'I know, Master. But even the dogs eat the scraps that fall from their master's table.'

²⁸'You've got great faith, haven't you, my friend! All right; let it be as you wish.'

And her daughter was healed from that moment.

One of the great moral and cultural issues of the last hundred years has been racial identity. The world was horrified to learn that the German Nazis had killed six million people whose only crime was to be Jews. The world was then increasingly horrified to watch as the apartheid system in South Africa discriminated in hundreds of ways against most of the population simply because of the colour of their skin. Eventually, through much hard work, change came. Other parts of the world still to this day make radical distinctions between peoples of different races.

But now, for many countries, the challenge is on: to take the widespread belief that all humans are equal, irrespective of race and colour, and to make this work within actual societies, where people from very different backgrounds can live together in peace and harmony. There is still much prejudice, much hatred, and much suspicion to be overcome.

So, when we read this story in our own setting, we may find it quite shocking. It looks as though Jesus, to begin with, is refusing to help someone in need just because she's from the wrong race. We wouldn't think much of a doctor or nurse who refused to treat a patient because they weren't from the right family background, or weren't the right colour. It seems very strange. What's going on?

We are here, once again, at a point where Jesus' fundamental mission is being defined. He wasn't simply a travelling doctor whose task was to heal every sick person he met. He had a very specific calling, which he already hinted at in 10.5–6. God's people, Israel, needed to know that their God was now at last fulfilling his promises. The **kingdom** for which they had longed was beginning to appear. He was its herald – and, as the **disciples** were starting to realize, he was himself God's anointed king.

But this **message** was always aimed at Israel itself. Not to maintain this would be to imply that God had made a mistake

199

in choosing and calling Israel to be his special people, the promise-bearers through whom his **word**, and his new life, would be brought to the rest of the world. Though many Christians, alas, have tried to forget the specialness of Israel in the purposes of God, the New Testament writers never do, and Jesus himself certainly never implied anything different. What he had come to do, as he says in Matthew 5, is not to abolish the **law**, but to fulfil it; not to do away with the category of 'Israel', God's chosen people, but to fulfil the purpose for which this people existed in the first place. If God's new life was to come to the world, it would come through Israel.

That's why Israel had to hear the message first. If the promise-bearing people were in danger of forgetting the promise, they must be reminded, precisely because the promises are now being fulfilled. If Jesus and his followers had simply begun an indiscriminate mission to the wider world, before God's purpose had unfolded, they would have made God a liar. That is why Jesus himself, and his followers at his instruction, limited their work almost entirely to the Jewish people.

But, as with so much of what happens in Jesus' public career, the future keeps breaking in to the present – even, as here, seeming to catch Jesus himself by surprise! He has already commented on the remarkable **faith** of a **Gentile** centurion (8.10); now he comments on the equally remarkable faith of a Canaanite woman, a non-Jew living some way north of the land of Israel. Jesus and his close associates had gone there, perhaps to escape any angry backlash from the controversial things he'd been saying and doing.

The Canaanite woman does indeed have great faith. Not only does she clearly believe that Jesus can heal her stricken daughter. She addresses Jesus as '**son of David**,' the Jewish messianic title which the disciples themselves were only gradually coming to associate with him. And, most remarkably, she understands, and uses to her advantage in the banter with Jesus, the way in which God's choice of Israel to be the promise-bearing people for the sake of the world was to work out in practice. Yes, she says, the dogs can't simply share the children's food. This is remarkable enough, that she accepts the designation 'dog', which was a regular way of dismissing the Gentiles as inferior. But she insists on her point. If Israel is indeed the promise-bearing people, then Israel's **Messiah** will ultimately bring blessing to the whole world. The dogs will share the scraps that fall from the children's table.

Of one thing we can be sure; the early church didn't make all this up. From very early on in the Christian movement the acceptance of Gentiles on equal terms with Jews was fought for within the church, and the battle was won, by Paul in particular. What we have here is as startling to us, perhaps, as it was to Jesus' followers at the time. The woman's faith broke through the waiting period, the time in which Jesus would come to Jerusalem as Israel's Messiah, be killed and raised again, and then send his followers out into all the world (28.19). The disciples, and perhaps Jesus himself, are not yet ready for Calvary. This foreign woman is already insisting upon Easter.

Being a Christian in the world today often focuses on the faith that badgers and harries God in prayer to do, now, already, what others are content to wait for in the future. In the early nineteenth century many Christians agreed that slavery was evil and would eventually have to stop, but not many wanted to do it just yet. William Wilberforce and his friends worked and prayed, devoting their lives to the belief that what would happen in the future had to happen, by God's power, in the present as well. That is the 'great faith' upon which Jesus congratulated this woman.

What, then, are the issues we face today? Which promises of God have we imagined might be fulfilled in the distant future, but ought to be claimed in the present with a prayer and faith which refuses to be put off?

MATTHEW 15.29–39

The Feeding of the Four Thousand

[29]Jesus went away from there, and arrived beside the sea of Galilee. He went up the mountain and sat down. [30]Large crowds came to him, with their lame, blind, crippled, mute and many others. They laid them at his feet, and he healed them. [31]When the crowd saw the mute speaking, the crippled made whole, the lame walking, and the blind seeing, they were astonished, and they gave praise to the God of Israel.

[32]Jesus called his disciples, and said, 'I am really sorry for the crowd. They've been around me now for three days and they haven't got anything to eat. I don't want to send them away hungry; they might faint on the way home.'

[33]The disciples said to him, 'Where could we get enough bread to feed a crowd this size, out in the country like this?'

[34]'How many loaves have you got?' asked Jesus.

'Seven,' they replied, 'and a few fish.'

[35]Jesus told the crowd to sit down on the ground. [36]Then he took the seven loaves and the fish, gave thanks, broke them, and gave them to the disciples, and the disciples gave them to the crowds. [37]And they all ate and were satisfied. And they picked up seven baskets full of what was left of the broken pieces. [38]There were four thousand men who had eaten, besides the women and children.

[39]Jesus sent the crowds away. Then he got into the boat and went over to the Magadan coast.

I went to the cinema the other day with my two nephews and niece. It wasn't an ordinary cinema. It was a three-dimensional production. Instead of looking at an ordinary movie, it seemed as though everything was coming out of the screen straight at you. Everybody shrieked as balls were thrown, water splashed, cars rushed out of the screen straight towards us. Cinemas like that were popular in the early days of movies, and they seem to be making a come-back, at least as a novelty for children.

Of course, for the three-dimensional trick to work you have to put on a special pair of spectacles, which the movie theatre supplies at the door. If you don't wear them, everything looks a bit blurred and you can't see the point. Once you're wearing them, you're part of the action and you can understand what's happening.

When you read any great literature you need to know what sort of spectacles to put on. I'm not talking about ordinary glass spectacles, the sort you may need to read with. I'm talking about the lenses you need to have inside your head if you're going to become part of the action, if you're going to understand what the writer is talking about and what it all really meant. This is true whether we're reading the Bible or Shakespeare, Goethe or Chaucer, or the great writers of our own day.

This passage in Matthew is an excellent case in point. Matthew tells us that the crowds brought to Jesus 'the lame, the blind, the cripples, and the mute'; and, when Jesus healed them, the crowd saw 'the mute speaking, the cripples being made whole, the lame walking, and the blind seeing'. He has already given us a good many stories of remarkable healings which Jesus performed. Why lengthen the book still further by adding these ones?

Put on the spectacles and you'll get the point. Matthew hopes that his readers will carry in their minds, as he undoubtedly did in his, many of the key prophetic texts from Israel's scriptures, the Old Testament. There are several texts that speak in beautiful poetry of the great time to come when God will rescue Israel from all its troubles. Here is one of the best known; Matthew intends us to 'see' the picture he is drawing in three dimensions by looking 'through' this text and others like it:

Then the eyes of the blind shall be opened
  and the ears of the deaf unstopped;
then the lame shall leap like a deer,
  and the tongue of the speechless sing for joy.

This text comes from the prophet Isaiah (35.5–6), and is part of a passage where God promises that the people of Israel will be brought back from **exile**, coming safely through the wilderness to arrive at their home. Matthew is underlining his belief that the long-awaited time is now at last coming to pass. The healings are not just signs of special, though peculiar, power. They are signs, three-dimensional signs if you like, of the fact that Jesus is fulfilling the old prophecies. Here, finally, is what Israel had been waiting for all along. No wonder he writes that the crowd 'gave praise to the God of Israel' (verse 31).

This may explain, too, why Matthew has included here a second story about Jesus feeding thousands of people in the wilderness, so soon after a very similar story in chapter 14. People have speculated about whether he sees any particular significance in the numbers (five thousand last time, four thousand this time; twelve baskets left over last time, seven baskets this time), but nobody has come up with a convincing explanation of what all this might mean. It has sometimes been suggested that the first feeding was intended to be of Jews, and the second of **Gentiles** (corresponding to verse 26, speaking of the children being fed before 'the dogs'), but there is no reason to suppose this crowd is either Gentile or in Gentile territory.

The important thing for Matthew, here as elsewhere, is that this takes place on a mountain (verse 29). Matthew makes many references in his **gospel** to another set of 'spectacles' which enable his readers to see what is going on in three dimensions: the 'Zion traditions', Old Testament prophecies in which Jerusalem ('Zion') would become the great mountain to which all the nations would flock to be saved. Only now it isn't Jerusalem to which everyone flocks, but Jesus himself; and he provides a feast for everyone who comes. What we have, then, is another way of saying what Isaiah 35 said: this is the time of fulfilment, the time when God's ancient promises to Israel were coming true.

And if that is so, it is also the time for the nations to come in and share the blessing. Think back to what we said about the Canaanite woman in the previous passage. She was pointing out that when God did for Israel what he was going to do for Israel, then the Gentiles would be included in the great feeding that would follow, even if for the moment it looked like dogs under the table eating what the children had dropped. This passage, then, looks ahead to the last mountain scene in the gospel, in 28.16–20, when Jesus sends his followers out into all the world to announce the **good news** of God's forgiving love to every creature.

Like all these stories, this one invites every single reader to live inside it and make it their own. We need to learn how to put on the appropriate spectacles. Matthew has given us several hints about these, and if we don't know the Old Testament well enough he will encourage us to read it more carefully so we can see the picture he is giving us in three dimensions. But we also need, through prayer and in fellowship with other readers today, to discover where the picture can become three-dimensional in our own world. Where in the world are the promises of God urgently needed today? Where are the sick and hungry still waiting for the blessing and hope of the one true God?

GLOSSARY

accuser, *see* **the satan**

age to come, *see* **present age**

apostle, disciple, the Twelve

'Apostle' means 'one who is sent'. It could be used of an ambassador or official delegate. In the New Testament it is sometimes used specifically of Jesus' inner circle of twelve; but Paul sees not only himself but several others outside the Twelve as 'apostles', the criterion being whether the person had personally seen the risen Jesus. Jesus' own choice of twelve close associates symbolized his plan to renew God's people, Israel (who traditionally thought of themselves as having twelve tribes); after the death of Judas Iscariot (Matthew 27.5; Acts 1.18) Matthias was chosen by lot to take his place, preserving the symbolic meaning. During Jesus' lifetime they, and many other followers, were seen as his 'disciples', which means 'pupils' or 'apprentices'.

baptism

Literally, 'plunging' people into water. From within a wider Jewish tradition of ritual washings and bathings, **John the Baptist** undertook a vocation of baptizing people in the Jordan, not as one ritual among others but as a unique moment of **repentance**, preparing them for the coming of the **kingdom of God**. Jesus himself was baptized by John, identifying himself with this renewal movement and developing it in his own way. His followers in turn baptized others. After his **resurrection**, and the sending of the **holy spirit**, baptism became the normal sign and means of entry into the community of Jesus' people. As early as Paul it was aligned both with the **Exodus** from Egypt (1 Corinthians 10.2) and with Jesus' death and resurrection (Romans 6.2–11).

Christ, *see* **Messiah**

circumcision

The cutting off of the foreskin. Male circumcision was a major mark of identity for Jews, following its initial commandment to Abraham (Genesis 17), reinforced by Joshua (Joshua 5.2–9). Other peoples, e.g. the Egyptians, also circumcised male children. A line of thought from Deuteronomy (e.g. 30.6), through Jeremiah (e.g. 31.33), to the **Dead Sea Scrolls** and the New Testament (e.g. Romans 2.29) speaks of 'circumcision of the heart' as God's real desire, by which one may become inwardly what the male Jew is outwardly, that is, marked out as part of God's people. At periods of Jewish assimilation into the surrounding culture, some Jews tried to remove the marks of circumcision (e.g. 1 Maccabees 1.11–15).

covenant

At the heart of Jewish belief is the conviction that the one God, YHWH, who had made the whole world, had called Abraham and his family to belong to him in a special way. The promises God made to Abraham and his family, and the requirements that were laid on them as a result, came to be seen in terms either of the agreement that a king would make with a subject people, or of the marriage bond between husband and wife. One regular way of describing this relationship was 'covenant', which can thus include both promise and law. The covenant was renewed at Mount Sinai with the giving of the **Torah**; in Deuteronomy before the entry to the Promised Land; and, in a more focused way, with David (e.g. Psalm 89). Jeremiah 31 promised that after the punishment of **exile** God would make a 'new covenant' with his people, forgiving them and binding them to him more intimately. Jesus believed that this was coming true through his **kingdom**-proclamation and his death and **resurrection**. The early Christians developed these ideas in various ways, believing that in Jesus the promises had at last been fulfilled.

David's son, *see* **son of David**

Dead Sea Scrolls

A collection of texts, some in remarkably good repair, some extremely fragmentary, found in the late 1940s around Qumran (near the north-east corner of the Dead Sea), and virtually all now edited, translated and in the public domain. They formed all or part of the library of a strict monastic group, most likely Essenes, founded in the mid-second century BC and lasting until the Jewish–Roman war of AD 66–70. The scrolls include the earliest existing manuscripts of the Hebrew and Aramaic scriptures, and several other important documents of community regulations, scriptural exegesis, hymns, wisdom writings, and other literature. They shed a flood of light on one small segment within the Judaism of Jesus' day, helping us to understand how some Jews at least were thinking, praying and reading scripture. Despite attempts to prove the contrary, they make no reference to **John the Baptist**, Jesus, Paul, James or early Christianity in general.

demons, *see* **the satan**

disciple, *see* **apostle**

Essenes, *see* **Dead Sea Scrolls**

eternal life, *see* **present age**

eucharist
The meal in which the earliest Christians, and Christians ever since, obeyed Jesus' command to 'do this in remembrance of him' at the Last Supper (Luke 22.19; 1 Corinthians 11.23–26). The word 'eucharist' itself comes from the Greek for 'thanksgiving'; it means, basically, 'the thank-you meal', and looks back to the many times when Jesus took bread, gave thanks for it, broke it, and gave it to people (e.g. Luke 24.30; John 6.11). Other early phrases for the same meal are 'the Lord's supper' (1 Corinthians 11.20) and 'the breaking of bread' (Acts 2.42). Later it came to be called 'the Mass' (from the Latin word at the end of the service, meaning 'sent out') and 'Holy Communion' (Paul speaks of 'sharing' or 'communion' in the body and blood of Christ). Later theological controversies about the precise meaning of the various actions and elements of the meal should not obscure its centrality in earliest Christian living and its continuing vital importance today.

exile

Deuteronomy (29—30) warned that if Israel disobeyed YHWH, he would send his people into exile, but that if they then repented he would bring them back. When the Babylonians sacked Jerusalem and took the people into exile, prophets such as Jeremiah interpreted this as the fulfilment of this prophecy, and made further promises about how long exile would last (70 years, according to Jeremiah 25.12; 29.10). Sure enough, exiles began to return in the late sixth century BC (Ezra 1.1). However, the post-exilic period was largely a disappointment, since the people were still enslaved to foreigners (Nehemiah 9.36); and at the height of persecution by the Syrians Daniel 9.2, 24 spoke of the 'real' exile lasting not for 70 years but for 70 *weeks* of years, i.e. 490 years. Longing for the real 'return from exile', when the prophecies of Isaiah, Jeremiah, etc. would be fulfilled, and redemption from pagan oppression accomplished, continued to characterize many Jewish movements, and was a major theme in Jesus' proclamation and his summons to **repentance**.

Exodus

The Exodus from Egypt took place, according to the book of that name, under the leadership of Moses, after long years in which the Israelites had been enslaved there. (According to Genesis 15.13f., this was itself part of God's covenanted promise to Abraham.) It demonstrated, to them and to Pharaoh, King of Egypt, that Israel was God's special child (Exodus 4.22). They then wandered through the Sinai wilderness for 40 years, led by God in a pillar of cloud and fire; early on in this time they were given the **Torah** on Mount Sinai itself. Finally, after the death of Moses and under the leadership of Joshua, they crossed the Jordan and entered, and eventually conquered, the Promised Land of Canaan. This event, commemorated annually in Passover and other Jewish festivals, gave the Israelites not only a powerful memory of what had made them a people, but also a particular shape and content to their **faith** in YHWH as not only creator but also redeemer; and in subsequent enslavements, particularly the **exile**, they looked for a further redemption which would be, in effect, a new Exodus. Probably no other past event so dominated the imagination of first-century Jews; among them the early Christians, following the lead of Jesus himself, continually referred back to the Exodus to give

210

meaning and shape to their own critical events, most particularly Jesus' death and **resurrection**.

faith

Faith in the New Testament covers a wide area of human trust and trustworthiness, merging into love at one end of the scale and loyalty at the other. Within Jewish and Christian thinking faith in God also includes *belief*, accepting certain things as true about God, and what he has done in the world (e.g. bringing Israel out of Egypt; raising Jesus from the dead). For Jesus, 'faith' often seems to mean 'recognizing that God is decisively at work to bring the **kingdom** through Jesus'. For Paul, 'faith' is both the specific belief that Jesus is lord and that God raised him from the dead (Romans 10.9) and the response of grateful human love to sovereign divine love (Galatians 2.20). This faith is, for Paul, the solitary badge of membership in God's people in Christ, marking them out in a way that **Torah**, and the works it prescribes, can never do.

Gentiles

The Jews divided the world into Jews and non-Jews. The Hebrew word for non-Jews, *goyim*, carries overtones both of family identity (i.e. not of Jewish ancestry) and of worship (i.e. of idols, not of the one true God YHWH). Though many Jews established good relations with Gentiles, not least in the Jewish Diaspora (the dispersion of Jews away from Palestine), officially there were taboos against contact such as intermarriage. In the New Testament the Greek word *ethne*, 'nations', carries the same meanings as *goyim*. Part of Paul's overmastering agenda was to insist that Gentiles who believed in Jesus had full rights in the Christian community alongside believing Jews, without having to become **circumcised**.

Gehenna, hell

Gehenna is, literally, the valley of Hinnom, on the south-west slopes of Jerusalem. From ancient times it was used as a garbage dump, smouldering with a continual fire. Already by the time of Jesus some Jews used it as an image for the place of punishment after death. Jesus' own usage blends the two meanings in his warnings both to Jerusalem itself (unless it repents, the whole city will become a smouldering heap of garbage) and to people in general (to beware of God's final judgment).

good news, gospel, message, word

The idea of 'good news', for which an older English word is 'gospel', had two principal meanings for first-century Jews. First, with roots in Isaiah, it meant the news of YHWH's long-awaited victory over evil and rescue of his people. Second, it was used in the Roman world for the accession, or birthday, of the emperor. Since for Jesus and Paul the announcement of God's inbreaking **kingdom** was both the fulfilment of prophecy and a challenge to the world's present rulers, 'gospel' became an important shorthand for both the message of Jesus himself and the apostolic message about him. Paul saw this message as itself the vehicle of God's saving power (Romans 1.16; 1 Thessalonians 2.13).

The four canonical 'gospels' tell the story of Jesus in such a way as to bring out both these aspects (unlike some other so-called 'gospels' circulated in the second and subsequent centuries, which tended both to cut off the scriptural and Jewish roots of Jesus' achievement and to inculcate a private spirituality rather than confrontation with the world's rulers). Since in Isaiah this creative, life-giving good news was seen as God's own powerful word (40.8; 55.11), the early Christians could use 'word' or 'message' as another shorthand for the basic Christian proclamation.

gospel, *see* **good news**

heaven

Heaven is God's dimension of the created order (Genesis 1.1; Psalm 115.16; Matthew 6.9), whereas 'earth' is the world of space, time and matter that we know. 'Heaven' thus sometimes stands, reverentially, for 'God' (as in Matthew's regular '**kingdom** of heaven'). Normally hidden from human sight, heaven is occasionally revealed or unveiled so that people can see God's dimension of ordinary life (e.g. 2 Kings 6.17; Revelation 1, 4—5). Heaven in the New Testament is thus not usually seen as the place where God's people go after death; at the end, the New Jerusalem descends *from* heaven *to* earth, joining the two dimensions for ever. 'Entering the kingdom of heaven' does not mean 'going to heaven after death', but belonging in the present to the people who steer their earthly course by the standards and purposes of heaven (cf. the Lord's Prayer: 'on earth as in heaven', Matthew 6. 10), and who are assured of membership in the **age to come**.

hell, *see* **Gehenna**

high priest, *see* **priest**

holy spirit

In Genesis 1.2, the spirit is God's presence and power *within* creation, without God being identified with creation. The same spirit entered people, notably the prophets, enabling them to speak and act for God. At his baptism by **John,** Jesus was specially equipped with the spirit, resulting in his remarkable public career (Acts 10.38). After his **resurrection**, his followers were themselves filled (Acts 2) by the same spirit, now identified as Jesus' own spirit: the creator God was acting afresh, remaking the world and them too. The spirit enabled them to live out a holiness which the **Torah** could not, producing 'fruit' in their lives, giving them 'gifts' with which to serve God, the world, and the church, and assuring them of future **resurrection** (Romans 8; Galatians 4—5; 1 Corinthians 12—14). From very early in Christianity (e.g. Galatians 4.1–7), the spirit became part of the new revolutionary definition of God himself: 'the one who sends the son and the spirit of the son'.

John (the Baptist)

Jesus' cousin on his mother's side, born a few months before Jesus; his father was a **priest**. He acted as a prophet, baptizing in the Jordan – dramatically re-enacting the **Exodus** from Egypt – to prepare people, by **repentance**, for God's coming judgment. He may have had some contact with the **Essenes**, though his eventual public message was different from theirs. Jesus' own vocation was decisively confirmed at his **baptism** by John. As part of John's message of the **kingdom**, he outspokenly criticized Herod Antipas for marrying his brother's wife. Herod had him imprisoned, and then beheaded him at his wife's request (Mark 6.14–29). Groups of John's disciples continued a separate existence, without merging into Christianity, for some time afterwards (e.g. Acts 19.1–7).

kingdom of God, kingdom of heaven

Best understood as the king*ship*, or sovereign and saving rule, of Israel's God YHWH, as celebrated in several Psalms (e.g. 99.1) and prophecies (e.g. Daniel 6.26f.). Because YHWH was the creator God, when he finally became king in the way he intended this would involve setting the world to rights, and particularly rescuing Israel from its enemies. 'Kingdom of God' and various equivalents (e.g. 'No king but God!') became revolutionary slogans around the time of Jesus. Jesus' own announcement of God's kingdom redefined these expectations around his own very different plan and vocation. His invitation to people to 'enter' the kingdom was a way of summoning them to allegiance to himself and his programme, seen as the start of God's long-awaited saving reign. For Jesus, the kingdom was coming not in a single move, but in stages, of which his own public career was one, his death and resurrection another, and a still future consummation another. Note that 'kingdom of **heaven**' is Matthew's preferred form for the same phrase, following a regular Jewish practice of saying 'heaven' rather than 'God'. It does not refer to a place ('heaven'), but to the fact of God's becoming king in and through Jesus and his achievement. Paul speaks of Jesus, as **Messiah**, already in possession of his kingdom, waiting to hand it over finally to the father (1 Corinthians 15.23–8; cf. Ephesians 5.5).

law, *see* Torah

legal experts, *see* Pharisees

leper, leprosy

In a world without modern medicine, tight medical controls were needed to prevent the spread of contagious diseases. Several such conditions, mostly severe skin problems, were referred to as 'leprosy', and two long biblical chapters (Leviticus 13—14) are devoted to diagnosis and prevention of it. Sufferers had to live away from towns and shout 'unclean' to warn others not to approach them (13.45). If they were healed, this had to be certified by a **priest** (14.2–32).

life, soul, spirit

Ancient people held many different views about what made human

214

beings the special creatures they are. Some, including many Jews, believed that to be complete, humans needed bodies as well as inner selves. Others, including many influenced by the philosophy of Plato (fourth century BC), believed that the important part of a human was the 'soul' (Gk: *psyche*), which at death would be happily freed from its bodily prison. Confusingly for us, the same word *psyche* is often used in the New Testament within a Jewish framework where it clearly means 'life' or 'true self', without implying a body/soul dualism that devalues the body. Human inwardness of experience and understanding can also be referred to as 'spirit'. *See also* **holy spirit**; **resurrection**.

message, *see* **good news**

Messiah

The Hebrew word means literally 'anointed one', hence in theory either a prophet, **priest** or king. In Greek this translates as *Christos*; 'Christ' in early Christianity was a title, and only gradually became an alternative proper name for Jesus. In practice 'Messiah' is mostly restricted to the notion, which took various forms in ancient Judaism, of the coming king who would be David's true heir, through whom YHWH would rescue Israel from pagan enemies. There was no single template of expectations. Scriptural stories and promises contributed to different ideals and movements, often focused on (a) decisive military defeat of Israel's enemies and (b) rebuilding or cleansing the **Temple**. The **Dead Sea Scrolls** speak of two 'Messiahs', one a priest and the other a king. The universal early Christian belief that Jesus was Messiah is only explicable, granted his crucifixion by the Romans (which would have been seen as a clear sign that he was not the Messiah), by their belief that God had raised him from the dead, so vindicating the implicit messianic claims of his earlier ministry.

miracles

Like some of the old prophets, notably Elijah and Elisha, Jesus performed many deeds of remarkable power, particularly healings. The **gospels** refer to these as 'deeds of power', 'signs', 'marvels', or 'paradoxes'. Our word 'miracle' tends to imply that God, normally 'outside' the closed system of the world, sometimes 'intervenes'; miracles have then frequently been denied by sceptics as a matter of principle. However, in the Bible God is always present, however strangely, and 'deeds of power' are seen as *special* acts of a *present* God rather than as *intrusive* acts of an *absent* one. Jesus' own 'mighty works' are seen particularly, following prophecy, as evidence of his messiahship (e.g. Matthew 11.2–6).

Mishnah

The main codification of Jewish law (**Torah**) by the **rabbis**, produced in about AD 200, reducing to writing the 'oral Torah' which in Jesus' day ran parallel to the 'written Torah'. The Mishnah is itself the basis of the much larger collections of traditions in the two Talmuds (roughly AD 400).

parables

From the Old Testament onwards, prophets and other teachers used various story-telling devices as vehicles for their challenge to Israel (e.g. 2 Samuel 12.1–7). Sometimes these appeared as visions with interpretations (e.g. Daniel 7). Similar techniques were used by the **rabbis.** Jesus made his own creative adaptation of these traditions, in order to break open the world-view of his contemporaries and to invite them to share his vision of God's **kingdom** instead. His stories portrayed this as something that was *happening*, not just a timeless truth, and enabled his hearers to step inside the story and make it their own. As with some Old Testament visions, some of Jesus' parables have their own interpretations (e.g. the sower, Mark 4); others are thinly disguised retellings of the prophetic story of Israel (e.g. the wicked tenants, Mark 12).

parousia

Literally, it means 'presence', as opposed to 'absence', and sometimes used by Paul with this sense (e.g. Philippians 2.12). It was already used in the Roman world for the ceremonial arrival of, for example, the emperor at a subject city or colony. Although the ascended Lord is not 'absent' from the church, when he 'appears' (Colossians 3.4; 1 John 3.2) in his 'second coming' this will be, in effect, an 'arrival' like that of the emperor, and Paul uses it thus in 1 Corinthians 15.23; 1 Thessalonians 2.19; etc. In the **gospels** it is found only in Matthew 24 (vv. 3, 27, 39).

Pharisees, legal experts, rabbis

The Pharisees were an unofficial but powerful Jewish pressure group through most of the first centuries BC and AD. Largely lay-led, though including some **priests**, their aim was to purify Israel through intensified observance of the Jewish law (**Torah**), developing their own traditions about the precise meaning and application of scripture, their own patterns of prayer and other devotion, and their own calculations of the national hope. Though not all legal experts were Pharisees, most Pharisees were thus legal experts.

They effected a democratization of Israel's life, since for them the study and practice of Torah was equivalent to worshipping in the **Temple** – though they were adamant in pressing their own rules for the Temple liturgy on an unwilling (and often Sadducean) priesthood. This enabled them to survive AD 70 and, merging into the early Rabbinic movement, to develop new ways forward. Politically they stood up for ancestral traditions, and were at the forefront of various movements of revolt against both pagan overlordship and compromised Jewish leaders. By Jesus' day there were two distinct schools, the stricter one of Shammai, more inclined towards armed revolt, and the more lenient one of Hillel, ready to live and let live.

Jesus' debates with the Pharisees are at least as much a matter of agenda and policy (Jesus strongly opposed their separatist nationalism) as about details of theology and piety. Saul of Tarsus was a fervent right-wing Pharisee, presumably a Shammaite, until his conversion.

After the disastrous war of AD 66–70, these schools of Hillel and Shammai continued bitter debate on appropriate policy. Following the further disaster of AD 135 (the failed Bar-Kochba revolt against Rome) their traditions were carried on by the rabbis who, though looking to the earlier Pharisees for inspiration, developed a Torah-piety in which personal holiness and purity took the place of political agendas.

present age, age to come, eternal life

By the time of Jesus many Jewish thinkers divided history into two periods: 'the present age' and 'the age to come' – the latter being the time when YHWH would at last act decisively to judge evil, to rescue Israel, and to create a new world of justice and peace. The early Christians believed that, though the full blessings of the coming age lay still in the future, it had already begun with Jesus, particularly with his death and **resurrection**, and that by **faith** and **baptism** they were able to enter it already. 'Eternal life' does not mean simply 'existence continuing without end', but 'the life of the age to come'.

priests, high priest

Aaron, the older brother of Moses, was appointed Israel's first high priest (Exodus 28—29), and in theory his descendants were Israel's priests thereafter. Other members of his tribe (Levi) were 'Levites', performing other liturgical duties but not sacrificing. Priests lived among the people all around the country, having a local teaching role (Leviticus 10.11; Malachi 2.7), and going to Jerusalem by rotation to perform the **Temple** liturgy (e.g. Luke 2.8).

David appointed Zadok (whose Aaronic ancestry is sometimes questioned) as high priest, and his family remained thereafter the senior priests in Jerusalem, probably the ancestors of the **Sadducees**. One explanation of the origins of the Qumran **Essenes** is that they were a dissident group who believed themselves to be the rightful chief priests.

rabbis, *see* Pharisees

repentance

Literally, this means 'turning back'. It is widely used in Old Testament and subsequent Jewish literature to indicate both a personal turning away from sin and Israel's corporate turning away from idolatry and back to YHWH. Through both meanings, it is linked to the idea of 'return from **exile**'; if Israel is to 'return' in all senses, it must 'return' to YHWH. This is at the heart of the summons of both **John the Baptist** and Jesus. In Paul's writings it is mostly used for **Gentiles** turning away from idols to serve the true God; also for sinning Christians who need to return to Jesus.

resurrection

In most biblical thought, human bodies matter and are not merely disposable prisons for the **soul**. When ancient Israelites wrestled with the goodness and justice of YHWH, the creator, they ultimately came to insist that he must raise the dead (Isaiah 26.19; Daniel 12.2–3) – a suggestion firmly resisted by classical pagan thought. The longed-for return from **exile** was also spoken of in terms of YHWH raising dry bones to new life (Ezekiel 37.1–14). These ideas were developed in the second-**Temple** period, not least at times of martyrdom (e.g. 2 Maccabees 7). Resurrection was not just 'life after death', but a newly embodied life *after* 'life after death'; those at present dead were either 'asleep', or seen as 'souls', 'angels' or 'spirits', awaiting new embodiment.

The early Christian belief that Jesus had been raised from the dead was not that he had 'gone to **heaven**', or that he had been 'exalted', or was 'divine'; they believed all those as well, but each could have been expressed without mention of resurrection. Only the bodily resurrection of Jesus explains the rise of the early church, particularly its belief in Jesus' messiahship (which his crucifixion would have called into question). The early Christians believed that they themselves would be raised to a new, transformed bodily life at the time of the Lord's return or **parousia** (e.g. Philippians 3.20f.).

sabbath

The Jewish sabbath, the seventh day of the week, was a regular reminder both of creation (Genesis 2.3; Exodus 20.8–11) and of the **Exodus** (Deuteronomy 5.15). Along with **circumcision** and the food laws, it was one of the badges of Jewish identity within the pagan world of late antiquity, and a considerable body of Jewish **law** and custom grew up around its observance.

sacrifice

Like all ancient people, the Israelites offered animal and vegetable sacrifices to their God. Unlike others, they possessed a highly detailed written code (mostly in Leviticus) for what to offer and how to offer it; this in turn was developed in the **Mishnah** (*c.* AD 200). The Old Testament specifies that sacrifices can only be offered in the Jerusalem **Temple**; after this was destroyed in AD 70, sacrifices ceased, and Judaism developed further the idea, already present in some teachings, of prayer, fasting and almsgiving as alternative forms of sacrifice. The early Christians used the language of sacrifice in connection with such things as holiness, evangelism and the **eucharist**.

Sadducees

By Jesus' day, the Sadducees were the aristocracy of Judaism, possibly tracing their origins to the family of Zadok, David's **high priest**. Based in Jerusalem, and including most of the leading priestly families, they had their own traditions and attempted to resist the pressure of the **Pharisees** to conform to theirs. They claimed to rely only on the Pentateuch (the first five books of the Old Testament), and denied any doctrine of a future life, particularly of the **resurrection** and other ideas associated with it, presumably because of the encouragement such beliefs gave to revolutionary movements. No writings from the Sadducees have survived, unless the apocryphal book of Ben-Sirach (Ecclesiasticus) comes from them. The Sadducees themselves did not survive the destruction of Jerusalem and the **Temple** in AD 70.

the satan, 'the accuser', demons

The Bible is never very precise about the identity of the figure known as 'the satan'. The Hebrew word means 'the accuser', and at times the satan seems to be a member of YHWH's heavenly council, with special responsibility as director of prosecutions (1 Chronicles 21.1; Job 1—2; Zechariah 3.1f.). However, it becomes identified variously with the serpent of the garden of Eden (Genesis 3.1–15) and with the rebellious daystar cast out of **heaven** (Isaiah 14.12–15), and was seen by many Jews as the quasi-personal source of evil standing behind both human wickedness and large-scale injustice, sometimes operating through semi-independent 'demons'. By Jesus' time various words were used to denote this figure, including Beelzebul/b (lit. 'Lord of the flies') and simply 'the evil one'; Jesus warned his followers against the deceits this figure could perpetrate. His opponents accused him of being in league with the satan, but the early Christians believed that Jesus in fact defeated it both in his own struggles with temptation (Matthew 4; Luke 4), his exorcisms of demons, and his death (1 Corinthians 2.8; Colossians 2.15). Final victory over this ultimate enemy is thus assured (Revelation 20), though the struggle can still be fierce for Christians (Ephesians 6.10–20).

scribes

In a world where many could not write, or not very well, a trained class of writers ('scribes') performed the important function of drawing up contracts for business, marriage, etc. Many scribes would thus be legal experts, and quite possibly **Pharisees**, though being a scribe was compatible with various political and religious standpoints. The work of Christian scribes was of initial importance in copying early Christian writings, particularly the stories about Jesus.

son of God

Originally a title for Israel (Exodus 4.22) and the Davidic king (Psalm 2.7); also used of ancient angelic figures (Genesis 6.2). By the New Testament period it was already used as a **messianic** title, for example, in the **Dead Sea Scrolls**. There, and when used of Jesus in the **gospels** (e.g. Matthew 16.16), it means, or reinforces, 'Messiah', without the later significance of 'divine'. However, already in Paul the transition to the fuller meaning (one who was already equal with God and was sent by him to become human and to become Messiah) is apparent, without loss of the meaning 'Messiah' itself (e.g. Galatians 4.4).

son of David

An alternative, and infrequently used, title for **Messiah**. The messianic promises of the Old Testament often focus specifically on David's son, for example 2 Samuel 7.12–16; Psalm 89.19–37. Joseph, Mary's husband, is called 'son of David' by the angel in Matthew 1.20.

son of man

In Hebrew or Aramaic, this simply means 'mortal', or 'human being'; in later Judaism, it is sometimes used to mean 'I' or 'someone like me'. In the New Testament the phrase is frequently linked to Daniel 7.13, where 'one like a son of man' is brought on the clouds of **heaven** to 'the Ancient of Days', being vindicated after a period of suffering, and is given kingly power. Though Daniel 7 itself interprets this as code for 'the people of the saints of the Most High', by the first century some Jews understood it as a **messianic** promise. Jesus developed this in his own way in certain key sayings which are best understood as promises that God would vindicate him, and judge those who had opposed him, after his own suffering (e.g. Mark 14.62). Jesus was thus able to use the phrase as a cryptic self-designation, hinting at his coming suffering, his vindication, and his God-given authority.

soul, *see* life

221

spirit, *see* **life, holy spirit**

Temple

The Temple in Jerusalem was planned by David (*c.* 1000 BC) and built by his son Solomon as the central sanctuary for all Israel. After reforms under Hezekiah and Josiah in the seventh century BC, it was destroyed by Babylon in 587 BC. Rebuilding by the returned **exiles** began in 538 BC, and was completed in 516, initiating the 'second-Temple period'. Judas Maccabaeus cleansed it in 164 BC after its desecration by Antiochus Epiphanes (167). Herod the Great began to rebuild and beautify it in 19 BC; the work was completed in AD 63. The Temple was destroyed by the Romans in AD 70. Many Jews believed it should and would be rebuilt; some still do. The Temple was not only the place of **sacrifice**; it was believed to be the unique dwelling of **YHWH** on earth, the place where **heaven** and earth met.

Torah, law

'Torah', narrowly conceived, consists of the first five books of the Old Testament, the 'five books of Moses' or 'Pentateuch'. (These contain much law, but also much narrative.) It can also be used for the whole Old Testament scriptures, though strictly these are the 'Law, prophets and writings'. In a broader sense, it refers to the whole developing corpus of Jewish legal tradition, written and oral; the oral Torah was initially codified in the **Mishnah** around AD 200, with wider developments found in the two Talmuds, of Babylon and Jerusalem, codified around AD 400. Many Jews in the time of Jesus and Paul regarded the Torah as being so strongly God-given as to be almost itself, in some sense, divine; some (e.g. Ben-Sirach 24) identified it with the figure of 'Wisdom'. Doing what Torah said was not seen as a means of earning God's favour, but rather of expressing gratitude, and as a key badge of Jewish identity.

the Twelve, *see* **apostle**

word, *see also* **good news**

YHWH

The ancient Israelite name for God, from at least the time of the

222

Exodus (Exodus 6.2f.). It may originally have been pronounced 'Yahweh', but by the time of Jesus it was considered too holy to speak out loud, except for the **high priest** once a year in the Holy of Holies in the **Temple**. Instead, when reading scripture, pious Jews would say *Adonai*, 'Lord', marking this usage by adding the vowels of *Adonai* to the consonants of YHWH, eventually producing the hybrid 'Jehovah'. The word YHWH is formed from the verb 'to be', combining 'I am who I am', 'I will be who I will be', and perhaps 'I am because I am', emphasizing YHWH's sovereign creative power.